THE AUTHOR'S ACCOUNTABILITY

PLANNER

A Day-by-Day Guide for Writers

"Because Writing is Hard."

2022

4 Horsemen
Publications, Inc.

4 Horsemen Publications, Inc.
1497 Main St. Suite 169
Dunedin, FL 34698
4horsemenpublications.com
info@4horsemenpublications.com

Authored by Erika Lance, JM Paquette, Valerie Willis, and Vanessa Valiente

Library of Congress Control Number: 2021947041

Paperback ISBN: 978-1-64450-339-3

DEDICATION

To all the great writers working on achieving
their dreams!

And those who joined the planner
family in 2021!

INTRODUCTION

"Guys, I need this in my life: An Author Accountability Guide."
The Researcher

"Yeah, we should do that!"   The Architect

"That's a great idea! Someone should do that!"
The Cheerleader

And so we became Someone.   The Taskmaster

Once upon a time, there were four Muses who decided to create a planner/ guide for writers. This magical book would be a new resource for those seeking to set goals, track progress (not just word count), and enjoy the Muse-inspired motivation to stick with it for an entire year. Thus, the Author's Accountability Planner was born.

We hope authors find this book useful through each stage of their writing journey. Writing and creating, whether full-time or part-time, require time and organization. This planner is designed to help track time, provide recommendations, and share what the Muses have discovered to be game changers on their own journeys.

Throughout the year, everyone faces the challenges of self-doubt, procrastination, and Life in General (Remember the 2020 pandemic jolting everyone around the globe? And it coming back in 2021!). It's okay! Every week, the Muses are here to guide you through this adventure.

We will get through this together.

HOW TO USE THIS BOOK

The Muses have spent countless hours fine-tuning the functionality of this book (by deciding if it should record writing time or beyond that). In the end, the Muses decided to account for all of the time spent doing writer-type things (brainstorming, writing, researching, editing, marketing, etc.). Many books discuss word count, but so much more happens before, after, and during the process of laying a book on paper (both physically and digitally).

Finishing the story is the single most important and difficult part of being a writer. To succeed, writers need accountability, someone or something to keep them motivated week after week. The Muses are here to keep the adventure moving forward, fight writer's block, and offer strategies to achieve year-end goals. Life is unpredictable, offering a variety of momentum-destroying reasons. This book can help you fight through those tough times while maintaining high morale.

In the end, only YOU can write YOUR story. You're here now, ready to do this. Let's go!

THE LAYOUT

This book contains four parts: Introductory Material (you're here!), Goal Setting, Month-by-Month Tracking, and Year Review. Each month has three sections: Monthly Prep, Weekly Overviews, and Monthly Review.

TRACKING DAILY ACCOMPLISHMENTS

Authors know that writing is more than sitting in a chair and putting words to paper (or screen). Word count is only one component of the writing process. A whole realm of prepping, marketing, research, and editing gets left out of all those other planners! We want you to be accountable by tracking all of the time you devote to your writing. Throughout this planner, the Muses have divided daily writing time into several different categories: Word Count, Brainstorming, Editing, Marketing, Research, and Reading.

Track your progress in these categories every day. It's okay to put a zero in a few places and focus on one task. Reviewing this information later can be

DAILY ACCOMPLISHMENTS	FRIDAY 29
Word Count:_____	Marketing Hours:_____
Brainstorming Hours:_____	Research Hours:_____
Editing Hours:_____	Reading Hours:_____

eye-opening when you compare good and bad weeks. In the end, use these pages to fine-tune your writing schedule, optimizing your output for all your writing needs. Some of us perform better when pairing tasks with one another; other times we reach higher word counts after reading and researching. Use these numbers to maximize your potential and make goal setting more rewarding.

WORD COUNT

You know this one! Word count is a common measure among authors to track their progress.

BRAINSTORMING

Some of us are pantsers while others are plotters. At times, we combine strategies! Either way, we spend some time prepping a story, even if it's an hour at the cafe writing on a napkin.

EDITING

Most writers work on more than one project at a time. Divide your attention between writing one work while editing another. One story might be completely drafted but still needs revision and editing. This step should never be skipped—whether posting to a blog or pitching to agents or publishers. Check your work.

MARKETING

If you dream to be famous, build awareness, or publish books, it's important to keep your author platform active by engaging on social media, writing blogs, posting advertisements, sending out newsletters, hosting events, and more. Automate as much as possible, scheduling your posts in advance to give yourself more time to create content. Don't risk losing your reader's interest!

RESEARCH

Whether researching how to buy a horse or a new method for writing dialogue, count your time. You're working! As a writer no less! These hours count too. ting. Some projects might be more demanding than others, so log your time!

READING

As writers, we hear this advice often: Read what you're writing! It's true! Read widely and often—both in and out of your comfort zone. Pick up a classic or treat yourself with the newest release. Engage in the writing world in every way.

I Want to Be a Writer

Take a look at all the projects and stories you want to complete for this coming year and predict your word count for them. It's okay to fall over or under—and you may massage these as the year progresses, but throw something out there to get started. Here's a rough scope of word counts to aid you in estimation:

TYPES	GENRE
Flash Fiction	Blog Posts
1,000 word or less	200-1,200
Short Story	Romance
1,200-10,000	50,000-70,000
Novelette	Paranormal
10,000-30,000	70,000-90,000
Novella	Fantasy
30,000-45,000	90,000-120,000
Novel	Crime
50,000-85,000	90,000-100,000
Epic Novel	Mystery/Thriller/Suspense
90,000-150,000	70,000-80,000
Textbook	Memoir
50,000-250,000	30,000-70,000
Young Adult	Science Fiction
50,000-80,000	90,000-125,000
Middle Grade	Horror
25,000-40,000	70,000-100,000
Chapter Books	Historical
10,000-20,000	80,000-120,000
Picture Books	Erotica
300-700	7,000-50,000

How many words will you write this year? _____

How many words did you complete last year? _____

How many projects will you complete? _____

SET THE OFFICIAL GOAL:

WHAT WILL YOU ACCOMPLISH THIS YEAR?

Congratulations on putting your goals into writing! You're committed to the adventure ahead. You're ready. Just a few more things while we're here.

Explain your motivation right now, in this moment, in words. Why are you doing this?

_____

_____

_____

_____

What goal(s) do you want to complete this year? Complete a novel, write a dozen short stories, or land an agent? Put it into the universe!

_____

_____

_____

_____

How are you going to accomplish this writing goal? No, really, literally write down how you will do this.

_____

_____

_____

_____

When will you be writing? (*Have set times in mind so you can establish a routine, but "whenever I can" is also a valid response! Get it done in whatever way works for you and your life.*)

_____

_____

_____

_____

Where will you be writing? (*Have you tried different places?*)

_____

_____

_____

_____

What do you need in order to write successfully? (*Fluff the pillow, cue the music, pour the drink, etc.*)

_____

_____

_____

_____

How will you be writing? (*computer, laptop, yellow legal pad, quill and ink pot, etc.*)

_____

_____

_____

_____

PLAN FOR PROBLEMS

*"He said we wouldn't get the treasure we seek on account of our
ob-stac-les."*

-Pete (Oh, Brother, Where Art Thou?)

D o some research and find writers who have experienced similar issues—what
did they do to succeed? How can you use their lives/experiences as a lesson
in your life?

Make a chart of obstacles that are within your control and those that are not.
When you feel yourself losing momentum or focus, refer to this chart to see how
you categorized the anti-writing forces in your life. If it's beyond your control,
then move on; there's nothing you can do about it. Do whatever you can to get
through this. But if it's something you said was controllable, think about what
you can do to adjust for the issue.

What are some obstacles that prevent you from writing?

_____

How can you overcome these issues?

_____

What has prevented you from writing in the past?

_____

How will you address these known pitfalls?

_____

DO OR DO NOT

*Do you wanna die having never been to Europe? Or do you
wanna go to Europe and die having been to Europe?*

Why are those my only two options?

- The Spy Who Dumped Me

T here is no try? Remember that you are not a jedi. Writing is not a done/not
done situation—because most writers would probably agree that writing is
never done, it's just due. It could always be better with one more round of edits,
one more polishing session, one more gentle nudge and subtle tweak.

Writing is a process, a journey, a path deeper into the woods. Use this book
to plan how far you'd like to travel along that path this year. As Tolkien said, the
road goes ever on and on, and we must follow if we can.

MOTIVATION TIME!

Are you motivated by rewards or punishment?

REWARDS: ALL OF THE PRIZES!

I'm the king of the world! —Jack (Titanic)

Does the idea of a sweet prize at the end of the road get you off your phone to write? It's time to reward yourself on top of the gloating satisfaction of sweet, sweet success.

WISH LIST TIME

You deserve all the things. Tease yourself with something really cool at the end of this road.

1ST PRIZE

Make it worthwhile—something to motivate you when you don't want to write. A long-desired trip, a fancy meal, a new leather-bound hardcover that you don't need but really really really want...shoot for the stars in your life!

What will you do for yourself when you reach your goal?

_____

2ND PRIZE

This should be something cool, something you wouldn't do or get for yourself normally, but not the magical rainbow party of 1st prize. You deserve this, but you could have had that other thing—use this feeling as motivation for next time!

What will you do for yourself when you get really close to your goal?

_____

3RD PRIZE

Again, make this something nice, worthwhile, but not the awesomeness you listed above. For me, 3rd prize would be like Chili's—slightly special/different and fun, but definitely not what I could have been eating right now.

What will you do for yourself when you get remotely close to your goal?

_____

HONORABLE MENTION

This should be a consolation prize, the webcam you win in the office give-away, the free pedometer from your insurance company, something new, but definitely not what it could have been.

What will you do for yourself for taking the first few steps toward your goal?

ALL OF THE PUNISHMENTS!

You can't handle the truth!

-Colonel Nathan R. Jessup (A Few Good Men)

Does the idea of an awful punishment push you out of bed to do some writing? It's time to envision the reckoning waiting for you if you fail. It's Negative Reinforcement Time: You want to accomplish your goals, but sometimes you need the threat of the blade over your neck to get it done. Threaten yourself with what will happen if you do not meet your goals. (It's really important that you set realistic goals if you plan to go this route!)

I COULD HAVE TRIED HARDER

You know it's true. It wasn't life getting in the way. It wasn't beyond your control. This is totally on you. What privilege should you lose as a result? Avoid choosing something writing-related as a punishment. Make it something you really don't want to do or deal with at all.

For example, if I blow a goal because of laziness, I have to take the stairs to my office at work. I work on the third floor, and the stairs are outside in the heat. The idea of trudging up them in the heat and humidity of a Florida summer is enough to get me out of bed and in front of my computer to write every day.

What will happen if you fail this way?

I PHONED IT IN

You know what happened. You were there, and you let it happen. You could have done it, but you did other things instead (not life-required things, but shiny objects that distracted you from your path). What privilege or perk should you lose? This could be something small to be a daily reminder of your failure or an all-in-one punishment that you'd rather not experience.

If I phone it in, I punish myself by wearing a really uncomfortable bra for a day or a week, depending on size of the goal/target. The discomfort is a constant reminder of my failure, motivating me the next time I think about phoning it in.

What should happen if you phone it in?

_____

_____

_____

I REALLY STOPPED TRYING

You know you topped even attempting to get it done. You let the magnitude of other things get in the way, and you didn't write what you wanted. (This is a good time to sit down and think about why you failed. Check out the I Failed... Now What? section). What privilege/perk should you lose for falling off the wagon? This should be more of a punishment than the previous two, something you really don't want to happen. For me, these are usually housework-cleaning related tasks. Bonus—I'm not allowed to return to my writing until my house is spotless.

What should happen if you really stop trying?

_____

_____

_____

I COMPLETELY GAVE UP

It happens. You walked away. But promises were made, and perhaps gifts were exchanged, and now you have to face the consequences. This should be serious, more than giving up your morning latte, beyond sweating over stairs or toilets. If you want the consequences method to work, this should be something you really really really don't want to experience.

Note—this isn't about berating yourself for failing, reinforcing how much you suck, or dwelling in how awful you are. Life happens. This punishment should be something you use as a proverbial sword over your neck to motivate you to write when you'd rather do anything else (even clean the toilet). My super awful worst punishment for not meeting a writing goal is living without music for an entire week. I love music—it's a huge part of my life and my makeup. I don't like a quiet house, a silent car ride, or a creepy echoing office in the evening after everyone goes home. Not having the option to cover the silence with sweet music is an awful possibility.

What should happen if you completely give up?

_____

_____

_____

Refer back to these pages periodically throughout the year. Remind yourself what you are working for—aside from the awesome, awe-inspiring feeling of finally completing a project that has haunted you for years, lingering in your brain unwritten for far too much of your life. You can totally do this!

MONTHLY PREP

Each month begins with planning—specific questions to make you think about the intersection between your writing and your life. Solid planning allows you to reach your goals.

For example, in November and December, writing time may be replaced with family time due to the holidays. It's okay to have smaller goals in the months with planned trips, scheduled events, or non-writing projects—when keeping normal routines is impossible. It's important for writers to be kind to themselves, finding that balance between accountability and self-flagellation.

LOOK AT YOUR MONTH

How many days this month will you work on writing stuff? Consider available weekdays/weekends. Will holidays affect your writing schedule? What is scheduled in your life that might affect your writing time? It's okay to plan for time when you will NOT write. Acknowledge your situation and plan accordingly.

What project(s) will you work on?

_____

_____

_____

Announcing your plan for the month is a special feeling. You can still stray if you want, but use this space to set your expectations (so you know what to prioritize this month).

What goal are you aiming to achieve?

_____

_____

_____

Now's your chance to assign a goal. Are you planning to finish a novel? Short story? Poem? Moving into the editing stage or brainstorming a new story by the end of the month? Goals can include sending out a set number of queries, gaining new followers, or buying that workbook you wanted.

What is your biggest obstacle this month?

_____

_____

_____

Anyone can look at a month and groan. Whether it's a holiday heavy month, the family reunion, or peak season with lots of overtime at your day job—we have all been there! Take a moment to acknowledge predictable obstacles.

How will you tackle these obstacles?

_____

_____

_____

Now, decide what you will do to address these issues. Will you bring a book to read and focus on a higher reading goal this month? Maybe lower your word count goal and double down on marketing since you can do social media from your phone while at a billion doctor appointments. You've got this!

What is your End of the Month reward?

_____

_____

_____

Treat yourself! It's hard following your dreams without some encouragement along the way. Life doesn't slow down, and you've made sacrifices to achieve your goals, so give yourself a pat on the back. Go to a movie, buy a new game, or even invite a friend over for wine and cheese. Always acknowledge how far you've progressed, even if not all your goals were met.

GOALS FOR THE MONTH

After this reflection time, you're ready to set your goals. It's okay to adjust them according to the demands of the month. Your monthly goals should be constantly evolving based on your previous month (that's why it's next to your Monthly Review).

WEEKLY OVERVIEW

Every week contains tasks, questions, and tips. After many painful choices, the Muses settled on what would be most helpful for your adventure this year: something to help with writer's block, remind you of your goals, and continue rewarding your creativity (perhaps with treats). Fill in this page during the week, and finish before moving on (Yes, this book has homework). Each item was chosen to prompt critical thinking and creativity on several levels.

EXERCISE

Every week, set a 5-minute timer and write a short work of fiction incorporating the two words. These short activities refill the creative well. Did you write something? Head over to the 4HP Accountable Authors Group on Facebook and share your awesome words!

QUESTIONS

WHAT WAS YOUR SPRINT TIME AND TOP WORD COUNT?

Was it a 20-minute sprint with 350 words? A 5-minutes dalliance with 75 words? You're awesome! Record it here.

LIST FAVORITE (OR NEW) SONGS YOU (RE)DISCOVERED THIS WEEK:

Writers have a toolbox that inspires us. What is the soundtrack for your current project? The Researcher and the Architect both have many playlists specific to their series to keep them fueled. Often, they exchange songs!

FAVORITE FOOD OR DRINK THIS WEEK:

What yummy food and drink did you have this week? Make sure you treat yourself on occasion. The Cheerleader enjoys trying out new teas, and the Taskmaster finds ways to reward not only herself, but fellow writers. Don't assume you have to do this alone. Eat and stay healthy. Self-care is critical. Don't neglect other parts of your life!

HOW DID YOU REWARD YOURSELF?

Not all of us enjoy food as a reward, so we ask...how did you reward yourself? Did you buy that item of clothing from that store? Order something cool online? Find another new book to read? Take a short trip outside? Oh, so many options here!

WHAT PROJECT(S) DID YOU ACTUALLY WORK ON?

Pay attention to which projects you work on. Sometimes one story will flow more easily than others. That's okay! Is there a pattern? Does a certain genre speak to you more than another? Seeing how many hours you devote to a specific project can be eye-opening.

WHAT ARE YOU READING RIGHT NOW?

Write down the titles of the books you read each week. Was it a writer resource? A reference book for brainstorming? Did you reward yourself with a cozy mystery? Remember to read, exposing yourself to other writers' words.

WHAT WENT WELL/COULD IMPROVE THIS WEEK?

Time to get real. Evaluate your strengths and troubleshoot your weaknesses at least once a week.

TOTALS FOR THE WEEK

Do some math. Bust out that calculator and punch it in. How did you do? Will this keep you on track to meet your monthly/yearly goals? See your progress stack up each month. Don't discredit anything! Writing is more than laying words to the page. You're not slacking when hours are spent on other facets of being an author!

MONTHLY JOURNAL

Visualize where you spend your time. See how much you are doing on average and how far you've made it this year! Write down your feelings on your progress. Let it out, shout it out, and put it out there! Remind yourself how far you've made it and how far you can take it.

MONTHLY REVIEW

To make it easier to find the month or circle back, we have put the month name and a color on the edge of the page. We feel it's SUPER important to look back and compare.

QUESTIONS

WHAT WAS YOUR TOP WEEK THIS MONTH?

There's so much that can happen in a month's time! Sit down and reflect. The Muses have pulled you into a conference room, and they're settling in to talk about how it's going (and the numbers). Don't worry—the Taskmaster is running the show, and she's already told the Researcher to focus. In fact, the Architect has pointed out some corrections while the Cheerleader is serving some tea (or coffee...or wine, depending on the month you've had).

WHAT MADE YOUR TOP WEEK SUCCESSFUL?

Looking back, it's always great to compare each week. Which one did you feel was top-notch? That's the kind of week you want to always have, one that leaves you feeling accomplished.

WHAT MADE YOUR TOP WEEK SUCCESSFUL?

What made that week so successful? Was it the reward or how you divide your time? Was there something you did differently? It's super important to be aware what made the difference so you have the ability to try to rinse and repeat.

WHAT WAS YOUR BIGGEST OBSTACLE?

Obstacles come in many varieties, big and small, controllable and uninvited. Acknowledge those mountains in your life and be mindful of how they influence your writing and creativity. This means you may have to change routine, maybe switch to more reading and brainstorming during these rougher climbs. It's about making your writing accountability work in your favor even in the toughest of times.

HOW DID YOU OVERCOME THIS? HOW COULD YOU IMPROVE NEXT MONTH?

Even if the answer is no, take a moment to consider strategies. Would it have been better to not worry about brainstorming and do editing or reading instead? These moments will help you tackle the next mountain.

WHAT WAS YOUR BIGGEST ACHIEVEMENT THIS MONTH?

Record the awesomeness! It can be anything and doesn't have to be something listed as a goal. Recognize what makes you feel good and boosts morale. Knowing what you can achieve makes for stronger goal setting next time.

WHAT INSPIRED YOU MOST THIS MONTH?

Inspiration comes from the most unexpected places. Track these for reference later down the road when you need a push or feel creativity slipping away. Was it a song? Something you saw in a show, movie, or documentary? Write it down! Come back to it and get recharged!

DID YOU DISCOVER A NEW WRITING TIP OR GREAT ADVICE THIS MONTH?

Writers are always learning. Advice comes in many forms, whether it's about actual writing or a fact about how to use social media in a nifty way. Write it down!

TOTAL FOR THE MONTH

Take the totals from your weeks and add those numbers up! How did you do? Did you meet a goal? Did you pass a goal? Did you not finish? These all help you plan better for the incoming month and set accurate goals.

TOTAL FOR THE YEAR

There's something satisfying about seeing how far you've come. Where are you in your journey? Do you need to adjust your weekly, monthly, or yearly goals? Don't be afraid to reassess goals. Life is unpredictable (Pandemic, anyone?). NEVER FEEL GUILTY! This is what good goal setting looks like and helps you stay on point!

Coloring Grids

Each month ends with a habit wheel you can color in as well as one for the end of the year! Don't feel obligated to color something in every day, and don't be afraid to cross out and write in other options when tracking habits. We've laid a foundation based on our own experience, but this is YOUR planner! Make it work for you so you can track and collect data to make you more accountable for the activities and habits you need as a writer.

MONTHLY GRID

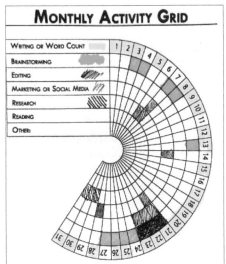

This grid is a visual graph to give you an idea which activity you favored in that month at a glance. It can also reveal if you have a tendency to "double up" tasks in the same day which can help you plan out and set new goals that match your tendencies. As you move through into a new year, looking back at these grids can help you plan for success in the years to come. Did you read a lot because of the holidays in December or was that due to other life events? Be sure to always use the journaling in conjunction to give Present You a reminder from Past You!

YEARLY GRIDS

In the back of this amazing planner, you will find not one, but two yearly grids. These grids provide a way to visualize your achievements this year. Not only do you get to pick the colors (fancy pen time!), but you can add a handful of non-writing activities to visually compare your hobbies. At the end of the year, you can see how your time shifts to favor specific activities, especially during months with holidays or life events. Recognizing these habits allows you to set stronger goals and understand how to adjust when needed. Seeing how your time is spent (and perhaps how it could be better used) can be a game changer. Also, knowing how long certain types of projects take to complete lets you plan more effectively next time.

BY ACTIVITY

We recommend coloring in the activity you did the most that day. If there's a tie, feel free to split the box into two colors! This is taking all that data you collected on yourself and giving you a visual graph for the year. Again, it's ok to have days that are blank! Self-care, life, and setting a schedule is about recognizing when you can't work on your writing and where you can make up for it in other months. This should give you an idea of when to plan for mostly writing or mostly editing, or realize that maybe you should do a hiatus in July because you don't get much done when you try due to summer time schedule changes! We all have that section or events that cause gaps and that's ok!

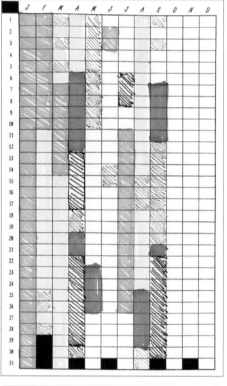

BY PROJECT

A project-based grid allows you to visualize how often you worked on a project, getting a sense of how much time you spent on a project. This grid can show how long it takes for you to work on different books or writing projects. Sometimes in our grids you see where we wrote the book and after a gap filled in by other projects, we circle back to edit that project! How long do you need to edit? And how long of a break seems to benefit you the most? Was there a time you didn't work on anything? These yearly maps of our lives as writers should help you in your coming year to plan for success. That doesn't mean you won't have to adjust and plan because like is often unpredictable!

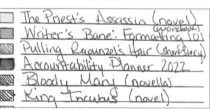

The Priest's Assassin (novel)
Writer's Bane: Formatting 101 (workbook)
Pulling Rapunzel's Hair (short story)
Accountability Planner 2022
Bloody Mary (novella)
King Incubus (novel)

THE MUSE PAGE

We can't leave you alone. That's why every week you get a little bit of something from each muse to help you through your 7-day struggle. The content here will change up often with a combination of inspirational quotes, exercises, fun facts, writing tips, and so much more. We hope we can make you smile, take a breath, and feel inspired to keep at it. This is hard work, we know! We're writers too! We want you to find your tribe and bring awareness of the writing community to all writers looking to connect and grow!

JOIN A WRITER'S COMMUNITY

First, we'd like to invite you to join the **4HP Accountable Authors Group on Facebook**. There. You now have joined an author's community filled with folks who are actively trying to stay accountable! Also, there's a lot of writers communities out there. Check with your local library, colleges and universities, cafes, writing associations, and more.

If you prefer online, many of these have options with a variety of hashtags on Twitter and Facebook by location and genre. Find workshops, classes, or give personal experience and advice. The greatest myth is the assumption that being a writer is a solitary ordeal. No. It's not. It doesn't have to be. Now, go into the light!

NANOWRIMO.ORG

We also highly recommend joining **NaNoWriMo.org** whether you are aiming to find your local writing tribe, connect with resources, or participate in the many novel writing events in November and during Camp NaNoWriMo throughout the year. Here are some things to note that NaNo does for all authors worldwide:

- Sponsor Writing workshops year-round, especially in October!
- Hosts a Forum where you can connect and get help from fellow writers!
- Encourage kinship as we all aim to write 50,000 words in a month.
- A means to track your writing and projects!
- Access to discounts for materials and services for authors.
- Discover local libraries, clubs, and peers who run your NaNo chapter!
- Alternatives to November and the ability to set smaller goals.
- A newsletter and social media to keep you connected and in-the-know.

The Cheerleader

Hello! So great to meet you! I love supporting writers! If you can't tell, I'm excited to have you here and for the opportunity to be your muse. My goal is to send you positive vibes, inspire your creativity, and encourage you to reward yourself often. Let's make magic happen!

I write paranormal romance and fantasy. Favorite Book: The Talisman by Stephen King and Peter Straub.

THE ARCHITECT

Your prose is beautiful, and I'm here to help you keep it polished and publishable. We are building your writing together, so look for my advice and reminders at every turn. This is about mastering your craft, and you don't have to do it alone. Let's build a masterpiece together!

I write young adult epic fantasy and adult paranormal romance.
Favorite Book: The Blue Sword by Robin McKinley

THE RESEARCHER

Did you know... that I love to drop facts and encourage you to discover new things outside your comfort zone. Stimulating the brain and sparking creativity through research and the world around you is a vital part of being a writer. Whether we're investigating some hidden nugget of history or looking back at how strange life can be, let's light a fire on your imagination.

I write fantasy, paranormal, mythology, romance, and erotica.
Favorite Book: The Captive Prince Trilogy

THE TASKMASTER

Staying focused and on point can be difficult. Oftentimes writer's block can derail days if not months of effort. I'm here to keep you on task! One way to do this is through constant evaluation and setting goals. I will be here to create a sense of urgency while keeping you moving forward in one way or another. Now, let's get to work!

I write horror, paranormal, thriller, and erotica.
Favorite Book: "YOURS! As soon as you finish it! Get to Work!"

Let the Accountability Planner Commence!

JANUARY

A new year has dawned, and the amazing muses are with you, ready to embark on this accountability adventure. As you take your first steps, remember the muses are here to encourage the process, enhance your skills, and eradicate your writing and editing woes. This adventure will help you set strong yet attainable writing goals this year.

Jan 1 New Year's Day
Jan 16 World Religion Day

*Jan 17 Martin Luther
King, Jr. Day*

*Jan 24 International Day
of Education*
Jan 30 World Leprosy Day

WHAT DOES YOUR MONTH LOOK LIKE

Holidays:_____   Weekends:_____

Weekdays:_____   Other:_____

What **project(s)** do you plan on working on?

_____

What **goal** are you aiming to achieve?

_____

What will be your biggest **obstacle** this month?

_____

How will you **overcome** this? Or adjust for this?

_____

What will be your End of the Month **reward**?

_____

GOALS FOR THIS MONTH

Word Count:_____   Marketing Hours:_____

Brainstorming Hours:_____   Research Hours:_____

Editing Hours:_____   Reading Hours:_____

JANUARY

Week 1

DAILY ACCOMPLISHMENTS   **SATURDAY 1**

Word Count: _____ *Marketing Hours:* _____

Brainstorming Hours: _____ *Research Hours:* _____

Editing Hours: _____ *Reading Hours:* _____

DAILY ACCOMPLISHMENTS   **SUNDAY 2**

Word Count: _____ *Marketing Hours:* _____

Brainstorming Hours: _____ *Research Hours:* _____

Editing Hours: _____ *Reading Hours:* _____

DAILY ACCOMPLISHMENTS   **MONDAY 3**

Word Count: _____ *Marketing Hours:* _____

Brainstorming Hours: _____ *Research Hours:* _____

Editing Hours: _____ *Reading Hours:* _____

DAILY ACCOMPLISHMENTS   **TUESDAY 4**

Word Count: _____ *Marketing Hours:* _____

Brainstorming Hours: _____ *Research Hours:* _____

Editing Hours: _____ *Reading Hours:* _____

DAILY ACCOMPLISHMENTS   **WEDNESDAY 5**

Word Count: _____ *Marketing Hours:* _____

Brainstorming Hours: _____ *Research Hours:* _____

Editing Hours: _____ *Reading Hours:* _____

DAILY ACCOMPLISHMENTS   **THURSDAY 6**

Word Count: _____ *Marketing Hours:* _____

Brainstorming Hours: _____ *Research Hours:* _____

Editing Hours: _____ *Reading Hours:* _____

DAILY ACCOMPLISHMENTS   **FRIDAY 7**

Word Count: _____ *Marketing Hours:* _____

Brainstorming Hours: _____ *Research Hours:* _____

Editing Hours: _____ *Reading Hours:* _____

WEEKLY OVERVIEW

Bubble   Tag

Post your exercise on the 4HP Accountable Authors Group on Facebook!

What was your sprint time and top word count?

_____

List a new song you discovered this week:

_____

Favorite food or drink this week:

_____

How did you reward yourself?

_____

What project(s) did you work on?

_____

What are you reading?

_____

What went well this week?

_____

What could improve this week?

_____

_____

_____

TOTAL FOR THE WEEK

Word Count:_____   Marketing Hours:_____
Brainstorming Hours:_____   Research Hours:_____
Editing Hours:_____   Reading Hours:_____

Don't forget to color in your grid!

JANUARY

The Cheerleader

Mark Twain decided to try his hand at fiction after reading a book by James Fenimore Cooper and deciding he could do it better. The world needs your voice!

THE ARCHITECT

Have you created a worldbook for your standalone/series? Even if you're writing in modern times, keep track of your characters by creating a reference guide. (i.e. religions, lakes, rivers, towns/cities, etc.)

THE RESEARCHER

Gift Time: What gifts would your characters appreciate? What gifts would they consider offensive?

THE TASKMASTER

As you start this journey remember: You have all the power to accomplish anything. Begin the journey and simply put one word in front of another.

JANUARY

WEEK 2

DAILY ACCOMPLISHMENTS   **SATURDAY 8**

WORD COUNT:_____   MARKETING HOURS:_____
BRAINSTORMING HOURS:_____   RESEARCH HOURS:_____
EDITING HOURS:_____   READING HOURS:_____

DAILY ACCOMPLISHMENTS   **SUNDAY 9**

WORD COUNT:_____   MARKETING HOURS:_____
BRAINSTORMING HOURS:_____   RESEARCH HOURS:_____
EDITING HOURS:_____   READING HOURS:_____

DAILY ACCOMPLISHMENTS   **MONDAY 10**

WORD COUNT:_____   MARKETING HOURS:_____
BRAINSTORMING HOURS:_____   RESEARCH HOURS:_____
EDITING HOURS:_____   READING HOURS:_____

DAILY ACCOMPLISHMENTS   **TUESDAY 11**

WORD COUNT:_____   MARKETING HOURS:_____
BRAINSTORMING HOURS:_____   RESEARCH HOURS:_____
EDITING HOURS:_____   READING HOURS:_____

DAILY ACCOMPLISHMENTS   **WEDNESDAY 12**

WORD COUNT:_____   MARKETING HOURS:_____
BRAINSTORMING HOURS:_____   RESEARCH HOURS:_____
EDITING HOURS:_____   READING HOURS:_____

DAILY ACCOMPLISHMENTS   **THURSDAY 13**

WORD COUNT:_____   MARKETING HOURS:_____
BRAINSTORMING HOURS:_____   RESEARCH HOURS:_____
EDITING HOURS:_____   READING HOURS:_____

DAILY ACCOMPLISHMENTS   **FRIDAY 14**

WORD COUNT:_____   MARKETING HOURS:_____
BRAINSTORMING HOURS:_____   RESEARCH HOURS:_____
EDITING HOURS:_____   READING HOURS:_____

JANUARY

EXERCISE: Take 5-minutes to write something with the 2 words below:

Banana   Jargon

Post your exercise on the 4HP Accountable Authors Group on Facebook!

What was your sprint time and top word count?

_____

List a new song you discovered this week:

_____

Favorite food or drink this week:

_____

How did you reward yourself?

_____

What project(s) did you work on?

_____

What are you reading?

_____

What went well this week?

_____

What could improve this week?

_____

_____

_____

TOTAL FOR THE WEEK

Word Count:_____   Marketing Hours:_____
Brainstorming Hours:_____   Research Hours:_____
Editing Hours:_____   Reading Hours:_____

Don't forget to color in your grid!

JANUARY

The Cheerleader

Socks vs bare feet while writing? What makes you comfortable?

THE ARCHITECT

Big Picture Time: What kind of project-wide issues are you facing right now? Think about how you can address these moving forward.

THE RESEARCHER

Remember The Giving Tree? Shel Silverstein was told this book would "never sell," and yet it became one of the most beloved children's books. Always see the dream through!

THE TASKMASTER

You are supposed to have started... Put your phone down and get off social media. You have a goal... Now get to it!

JANUARY

DAILY ACCOMPLISHMENTS   **SATURDAY 15**

*Word Count:*_____   *Marketing Hours:*_____
*Brainstorming Hours:*_____   *Research Hours:*_____
*Editing Hours:*_____   *Reading Hours:*_____

DAILY ACCOMPLISHMENTS   **SUNDAY 16**

*Word Count:*_____   *Marketing Hours:*_____
*Brainstorming Hours:*_____   *Research Hours:*_____
*Editing Hours:*_____   *Reading Hours:*_____

DAILY ACCOMPLISHMENTS   **MONDAY 17**

*Word Count:*_____   *Marketing Hours:*_____
*Brainstorming Hours:*_____   *Research Hours:*_____
*Editing Hours:*_____   *Reading Hours:*_____

DAILY ACCOMPLISHMENTS   **TUESDAY 18**

*Word Count:*_____   *Marketing Hours:*_____
*Brainstorming Hours:*_____   *Research Hours:*_____
*Editing Hours:*_____   *Reading Hours:*_____

DAILY ACCOMPLISHMENTS   **WEDNESDAY 19**

*Word Count:*_____   *Marketing Hours:*_____
*Brainstorming Hours:*_____   *Research Hours:*_____
*Editing Hours:*_____   *Reading Hours:*_____

DAILY ACCOMPLISHMENTS   **THURSDAY 20**

*Word Count:*_____   *Marketing Hours:*_____
*Brainstorming Hours:*_____   *Research Hours:*_____
*Editing Hours:*_____   *Reading Hours:*_____

DAILY ACCOMPLISHMENTS   **FRIDAY 21**

*Word Count:*_____   *Marketing Hours:*_____
*Brainstorming Hours:*_____   *Research Hours:*_____
*Editing Hours:*_____   *Reading Hours:*_____

EXERCISE: Take 5-minutes to write something with the 2 words below:

Ghost   Holiday

Post your exercise on the 4HP Accountable Authors Group on Facebook!

What was your sprint time and top word count?

_____

List a new song you discovered this week:

_____

Favorite food or drink this week:

_____

How did you reward yourself?

_____

What project(s) did you work on?

_____

What are you reading?

_____

What went well this week?

_____

What could improve this week?

_____

_____

_____

TOTAL FOR THE WEEK

Word Count:_____   Marketing Hours:_____
Brainstorming Hours:_____   Research Hours:_____
Editing Hours:_____   Reading Hours:_____

Don't forget to color in your grid!

JANUARY

The Cheerleader

Almost there! Give yourself some encouragement as the finish line creeps into view.

THE ARCHITECT

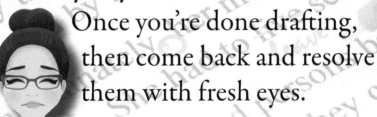

Leave notes/comments as you draft your story so you don't lose momentum. Once you're done drafting, then come back and resolve them with fresh eyes.

THE RESEARCHER

"The idea is to write it so people hear it, and it slides through the brain and goes straight to the heart."

~ Maya Angelou

THE TASKMASTER

"Never give up! Never surrender!"

~ Jason Nesmith (Galaxy Quest)

Make this quote your mantra. Keep going no matter what happens.

JANUARY

DAILY ACCOMPLISHMENTS   **SATURDAY 22**

WORD COUNT:_____   MARKETING HOURS:_____
BRAINSTORMING HOURS:_____ RESEARCH HOURS:_____
EDITING HOURS:_____   READING HOURS:_____

DAILY ACCOMPLISHMENTS   **SUNDAY 23**

WORD COUNT:_____   MARKETING HOURS:_____
BRAINSTORMING HOURS:_____ RESEARCH HOURS:_____
EDITING HOURS:_____   READING HOURS:_____

DAILY ACCOMPLISHMENTS   **MONDAY 24**

WORD COUNT:_____   MARKETING HOURS:_____
BRAINSTORMING HOURS:_____ RESEARCH HOURS:_____
EDITING HOURS:_____   READING HOURS:_____

DAILY ACCOMPLISHMENTS   **TUESDAY 25**

WORD COUNT:_____   MARKETING HOURS:_____
BRAINSTORMING HOURS:_____ RESEARCH HOURS:_____
EDITING HOURS:_____   READING HOURS:_____

DAILY ACCOMPLISHMENTS   **WEDNESDAY 26**

WORD COUNT:_____   MARKETING HOURS:_____
BRAINSTORMING HOURS:_____ RESEARCH HOURS:_____
EDITING HOURS:_____   READING HOURS:_____

DAILY ACCOMPLISHMENTS   **THURSDAY 27**

WORD COUNT:_____   MARKETING HOURS:_____
BRAINSTORMING HOURS:_____ RESEARCH HOURS:_____
EDITING HOURS:_____   READING HOURS:_____

DAILY ACCOMPLISHMENTS   **FRIDAY 28**

WORD COUNT:_____   MARKETING HOURS:_____
BRAINSTORMING HOURS:_____ RESEARCH HOURS:_____
EDITING HOURS:_____   READING HOURS:_____

JANUARY

WEEKLY OVERVIEW

EXERCISE: Take 5-minutes to write something with the 2 words below:

Summon   Wax

Post your exercise on the 4HP Accountable Authors Group on Facebook!

What was your sprint time and top word count?

_____

List a new song you discovered this week:

_____

Favorite food or drink this week:

_____

How did you reward yourself?

_____

What project(s) did you work on?

_____

What are you reading?

_____

What went well this week?

_____

What could improve this week?

_____

_____

_____

TOTAL FOR THE WEEK

Word Count:_____   Marketing Hours:_____
Brainstorming Hours:_____   Research Hours:_____
Editing Hours:_____   Reading Hours:_____

Don't forget to color in your grid!

The Cheerleader

"It's not the years, honey. It's the mileage." ~ Indiana Jones

THE ARCHITECT

Read your writing out loud. It's a great way to discover errors and inconsistencies in your prose.

THE RESEARCHER

Cats are mischievious and fun companions for characters. During the 13th Century, Pope Gregory IV declared war on cats, beginning the association of black cats with Satan! As a result, the plague spiked...

THE TASKMASTER

"If you want to change the world, pick up your pen and write."
~ *Martin Luther King*

Right now is your chance to change the world. I know you are up to the task.

January

DAILY ACCOMPLISHMENTS   **SATURDAY 29**

WORD COUNT:_____

BRAINSTORMING HOURS:_____

EDITING HOURS:_____

MARKETING HOURS:_____

RESEARCH HOURS:_____

READING HOURS:_____

DAILY ACCOMPLISHMENTS   **SUNDAY 30**

WORD COUNT:_____

BRAINSTORMING HOURS:_____

EDITING HOURS:_____

MARKETING HOURS:_____

RESEARCH HOURS:_____

READING HOURS:_____

DAILY ACCOMPLISHMENTS   **MONDAY 31**

WORD COUNT:_____

BRAINSTORMING HOURS:_____

EDITING HOURS:_____

MARKETING HOURS:_____

RESEARCH HOURS:_____

READING HOURS:_____

THE TASKMASTER

It is the start of your epic adventure. You may be feeling a little nervous, a bit excited, and most especially, certain you are going to rule the world by the end of 2022. Remember, you can be your own worst enemy. Get out of your own way.

Weekly Overview

Plan   Steak

Post your exercise on the 4HP Accountable Authors Group on Facebook!

What was your sprint time and top word count?

_____

List a new song you discovered this week:

_____

Favorite food or drink this week:

_____

How did you reward yourself?

_____

What project(s) did you work on?

_____

What are you reading?

_____

What went well this week?

_____

What could improve this week?

_____

_____

_____

Total for the Week

Word Count:_____   Marketing Hours:_____
Brainstorming Hours:_____   Research Hours:_____
Editing Hours:_____   Reading Hours:_____

Don't forget to color in your grid!

JANUARY

MONTHLY ACTIVITY GRID

JANUARY

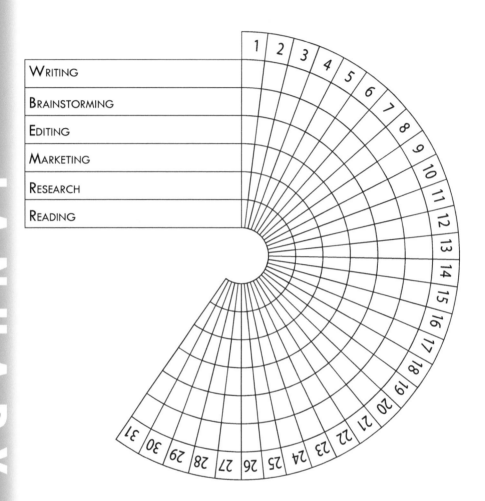

WRITING

BRAINSTORMING

EDITING

MARKETING

RESEARCH

READING

YOUR AVERAGE WORD COUNT FOR THE MONTH

Total Word Count:_____ Divided by _____ days =_____

TOTAL FOR THE YEAR SO FAR

Word Count:_____   Marketing Hours:_____
Brainstorming Hours:_____   Research Hours:_____
Editing Hours:_____   Reading Hours:_____

JOURNAL

JANUARY

What was your **top week**?

_____

What made your **top week** successful?

_____

What was your biggest **obstacle**?

_____

How did you **overcome** this? Or could do better next time?

_____

_____

What was your biggest **achievement**?

_____

_____

What **inspired** you most this month?

_____

Did you **discover** a new writing tip or advice this month?

_____

_____

TOTAL FOR THE MONTH

Word Count:_____   Research Hours:_____
Brainstorming Hours:_____   Reading Hours:_____
Editing Hours:_____
Marketing Hours:_____

TOTAL FOR THE YEAR SO FAR

Word Count:_____   Research Hours:_____
Brainstorming Hours:_____   Reading Hours:_____
Editing Hours:_____
Marketing Hours:_____

Don't forget to color in your grid!

FEBRUARY

As you begin month two of this adventure, you should start to find your routine. Experts say it takes six weeks to develop a habit. Do not forget that this is your journey, and February is the month of love. Make sure you are loving yourself!

Black History Month
Feb 1 Chinese New Year
Feb 2 Groundhog Day

Feb 4 National
Wear Red Day

Feb 14 Valentine's Day
Feb 21 President's Day

WHAT DOES YOUR MONTH LOOK LIKE

Holidays:_____   Weekends:_____
Weekdays:_____   Other:_____

What **project(s)** do you plan on working on?

_____

What **goal** are you aiming to achieve?

_____

What will be your biggest **obstacle** this month?

_____

How will you **overcome** this? Or adjust for this?

_____

What will be your End of the Month **reward**?

_____

GOALS FOR THIS MONTH

Word Count:_____   Marketing Hours:_____
Brainstorming Hours:_____   Research Hours:_____
Editing Hours:_____   Reading Hours:_____

23

Week 1

FEBRUARY

DAILY ACCOMPLISHMENTS   TUESDAY 1

Word Count: _____
Brainstorming Hours: _____
Editing Hours: _____

Marketing Hours: _____
Research Hours: _____
Reading Hours: _____

DAILY ACCOMPLISHMENTS   WEDNESDAY 2

Word Count: _____
Brainstorming Hours: _____
Editing Hours: _____

Marketing Hours: _____
Research Hours: _____
Reading Hours: _____

DAILY ACCOMPLISHMENTS   THURSDAY 3

Word Count: _____
Brainstorming Hours: _____
Editing Hours: _____

Marketing Hours: _____
Research Hours: _____
Reading Hours: _____

DAILY ACCOMPLISHMENTS   FRIDAY 4

Word Count: _____
Brainstorming Hours: _____
Editing Hours: _____

Marketing Hours: _____
Research Hours: _____
Reading Hours: _____

DAILY ACCOMPLISHMENTS   SATURDAY 5

Word Count: _____
Brainstorming Hours: _____
Editing Hours: _____

Marketing Hours: _____
Research Hours: _____
Reading Hours: _____

DAILY ACCOMPLISHMENTS   SUNDAY 6

Word Count: _____
Brainstorming Hours: _____
Editing Hours: _____

Marketing Hours: _____
Research Hours: _____
Reading Hours: _____

DAILY ACCOMPLISHMENTS   MONDAY 7

Word Count: _____
Brainstorming Hours: _____
Editing Hours: _____

Marketing Hours: _____
Research Hours: _____
Reading Hours: _____

24

WEEKLY OVERVIEW

Creepy   Athlete

Post your exercise on the 4HP Accountable Authors Group on Facebook!

What was your sprint time and top word count?

_____

List a new song you discovered this week:

_____

Favorite food or drink this week:

_____

How did you reward yourself?

_____

What project(s) did you work on?

_____

What are you reading?

_____

What went well this week?

_____

What could improve this week?

_____

_____

_____

TOTAL FOR THE WEEK

Word Count:_____   Marketing Hours:_____
Brainstorming Hours:_____   Research Hours:_____
Editing Hours:_____   Reading Hours:_____

Don't forget to color in your grid!

FEBRUARY

FEBRUARY

The Cheerleader

What's your favorite book of all time? Why?

THE ARCHITECT

"Exercise the writing muscle every day, even if it is only a letter, notes, a title list, a character sketch, a journal entry. Writers are like dancers, like athletes. Without that exercise, the muscles seize up."

~ *Jane Yolen*

THE RESEARCHER

Herman Melville recieved a rejection that said Moby Dick would be better if he took the whale out and that his story was too long and too old fashioned... and here we are in 2022 still reading it! HA!

THE TASKMASTER

When did you last change your author photo or background image on social media? Do it now!

FEBRUARY

DAILY ACCOMPLISHMENTS   **TUESDAY 8**

Word Count: _____ *Marketing Hours:* _____
Brainstorming Hours: _____ *Research Hours:* _____
Editing Hours: _____ *Reading Hours:* _____

DAILY ACCOMPLISHMENTS   **WEDNESDAY 9**

Word Count: _____ *Marketing Hours:* _____
Brainstorming Hours: _____ *Research Hours:* _____
Editing Hours: _____ *Reading Hours:* _____

DAILY ACCOMPLISHMENTS   **THURSDAY 10**

Word Count: _____ *Marketing Hours:* _____
Brainstorming Hours: _____ *Research Hours:* _____
Editing Hours: _____ *Reading Hours:* _____

DAILY ACCOMPLISHMENTS   **FRIDAY 11**

Word Count: _____ *Marketing Hours:* _____
Brainstorming Hours: _____ *Research Hours:* _____
Editing Hours: _____ *Reading Hours:* _____

DAILY ACCOMPLISHMENTS   **SATURDAY 12**

Word Count: _____ *Marketing Hours:* _____
Brainstorming Hours: _____ *Research Hours:* _____
Editing Hours: _____ *Reading Hours:* _____

DAILY ACCOMPLISHMENTS   **SUNDAY 13**

Word Count: _____ *Marketing Hours:* _____
Brainstorming Hours: _____ *Research Hours:* _____
Editing Hours: _____ *Reading Hours:* _____

DAILY ACCOMPLISHMENTS   **MONDAY 14**

Word Count: _____ *Marketing Hours:* _____
Brainstorming Hours: _____ *Research Hours:* _____
Editing Hours: _____ *Reading Hours:* _____

FEBRUARY

WEEKLY OVERVIEW

EXERCISE: Take 5-minutes to write something with the 2 words below:

Wind   Shoes

Post your exercise on the 4HP Accountable Authors Group on Facebook!

What was your sprint time and top word count?

_____

List a new song you discovered this week:

_____

Favorite food or drink this week:

_____

How did you reward yourself?

_____

What project(s) did you work on?

_____

What are you reading?

_____

What went well this week?

_____

What could improve this week?

_____

_____

_____

TOTAL FOR THE WEEK

Word Count:_____   Marketing Hours:_____
Brainstorming Hours:_____   Research Hours:_____
Editing Hours:_____   Reading Hours:_____

Don't forget to color in your grid!

The Cheerleader

Who inspires you right now? Why? Who inspires your characters?

THE ARCHITECT

"The unread story is not a story; it is little black marks on wood pulp. The reader, reading it, makes it live: a live thing, a story."

~ Ursula K. Le Guin

THE RESEARCHER

Choose one below to research. Set a timer for 20 minutes and write a story or character inspired by something you've learned.
1) British "Unkillable" Soldier, Adrian Carton de Wiart

THE TASKMASTER

Find a podcast (We recommend Drinking with Authors). Listen to it as you go outside and walk. Exercise is important.

FEBRUARY

WEEK 3

DAILY ACCOMPLISHMENTS	TUESDAY 15
WORD COUNT:	MARKETING HOURS:
BRAINSTORMING HOURS:	RESEARCH HOURS:
EDITING HOURS:	READING HOURS:

DAILY ACCOMPLISHMENTS	WEDNESDAY 16
WORD COUNT:	MARKETING HOURS:
BRAINSTORMING HOURS:	RESEARCH HOURS:
EDITING HOURS:	READING HOURS:

DAILY ACCOMPLISHMENTS	THURSDAY 17
WORD COUNT:	MARKETING HOURS:
BRAINSTORMING HOURS:	RESEARCH HOURS:
EDITING HOURS:	READING HOURS:

DAILY ACCOMPLISHMENTS	FRIDAY 18
WORD COUNT:	MARKETING HOURS:
BRAINSTORMING HOURS:	RESEARCH HOURS:
EDITING HOURS:	READING HOURS:

DAILY ACCOMPLISHMENTS	SATURDAY 19
WORD COUNT:	MARKETING HOURS:
BRAINSTORMING HOURS:	RESEARCH HOURS:
EDITING HOURS:	READING HOURS:

DAILY ACCOMPLISHMENTS	SUNDAY 20
WORD COUNT:	MARKETING HOURS:
BRAINSTORMING HOURS:	RESEARCH HOURS:
EDITING HOURS:	READING HOURS:

DAILY ACCOMPLISHMENTS	MONDAY 21
WORD COUNT:	MARKETING HOURS:
BRAINSTORMING HOURS:	RESEARCH HOURS:
EDITING HOURS:	READING HOURS:

WEEKLY OVERVIEW

EXERCISE: Take 5-minutes to write something with the 2 words below:

Amuse   Mist

Post your exercise on the 4HP Accountable Authors Group on Facebook!

What was your sprint time and top word count?

_____

List a new song you discovered this week:

_____

Favorite food or drink this week:

_____

How did you reward yourself?

_____

What project(s) did you work on?

_____

What are you reading?

_____

What went well this week?

_____

What could improve this week?

_____

_____

_____

TOTAL FOR THE WEEK

Word Count:_____   Marketing Hours:_____
Brainstorming Hours:_____   Research Hours:_____
Editing Hours:_____   Reading Hours:_____

Don't forget to color in your grid!

33

FEBRUARY

The Cheerleader

An author finally landed a publishing contract after 5 years of continual rejections. Who? Agatha Christie who has sold over $2 billion in books!

THE ARCHITECT

Keep an eye out for "was." Rephrase the sentence to use more active verbs. Example: She was walking across the street. Alternative: She walked across the street. She strode across the street. She strut her stuff across the pavement.

THE RESEARCHER

When Paulo Coelho's publisher gave the rights back to him for The Alchemist after only a year, he went on a 40-day excursion in the Mojave Desert. He returned and decided he would continue to struggle. He knocked door-to-door and now his book has

THE TASKMASTER

Strike a balance between showing and telling. Unless you're writing a book about trees, or it's a vital detail to the story, nobody cares about three paragraphs describing the shape of a leaf. Find this crap and remove it. (Tolkien has strong feelings about this.)

FEBRUARY

WEEK 4

DAILY ACCOMPLISHMENTS	**TUESDAY 22**
Word Count:	*Marketing Hours:*
Brainstorming Hours:	*Research Hours:*
Editing Hours:	*Reading Hours:*

DAILY ACCOMPLISHMENTS	**WEDNESDAY 23**
Word Count:	*Marketing Hours:*
Brainstorming Hours:	*Research Hours:*
Editing Hours:	*Reading Hours:*

DAILY ACCOMPLISHMENTS	**THURSDAY 24**
Word Count:	*Marketing Hours:*
Brainstorming Hours:	*Research Hours:*
Editing Hours:	*Reading Hours:*

DAILY ACCOMPLISHMENTS	**FRIDAY 25**
Word Count:	*Marketing Hours:*
Brainstorming Hours:	*Research Hours:*
Editing Hours:	*Reading Hours:*

DAILY ACCOMPLISHMENTS	**SATURDAY 26**
Word Count:	*Marketing Hours:*
Brainstorming Hours:	*Research Hours:*
Editing Hours:	*Reading Hours:*

DAILY ACCOMPLISHMENTS	**SUNDAY 27**
Word Count:	*Marketing Hours:*
Brainstorming Hours:	*Research Hours:*
Editing Hours:	*Reading Hours:*

DAILY ACCOMPLISHMENTS	**MONDAY 28**
Word Count:	*Marketing Hours:*
Brainstorming Hours:	*Research Hours:*
Editing Hours:	*Reading Hours:*

WEEKLY OVERVIEW

What was your sprint time and top word count?

_____

List a new song you discovered this week:

_____

Favorite food or drink this week:

_____

How did you reward yourself?

_____

What project(s) did you work on?

_____

What are you reading?

_____

What went well this week?

_____

What could improve this week?

_____

_____

_____

TOTAL FOR THE WEEK

Word Count:_____   Marketing Hours:_____
Brainstorming Hours:_____   Research Hours:_____
Editing Hours:_____   Reading Hours:_____

Don't forget to color in your grid!

FEBRUARY

The Cheerleader

5 Minute Outline Break: Outline a project that you're thinking about. Set a timer.

THE ARCHITECT

"A writer is someone for whom writing is more difficult than it is for other people."
~ *Thomas Mann, Essays of Three Decades*

FEBRUARY

THE RESEARCHER

If you can find a local or virtual open mic, go share and test material! You never know who might be there! For example, Mark Twain had no idea that his lecture about that time he stole a watermelon as a kid was attended by Sigmund Freud!

THE TASKMASTER

"It's the job that's never started that takes the longest to finish."

~ Samwise Gamgee (Lord of the Rings)

You need to be writing every single day, even if it is only for 20 minutes.

FEBRUARY

MONTHLY ACTIVITY GRID

FEBRUARY

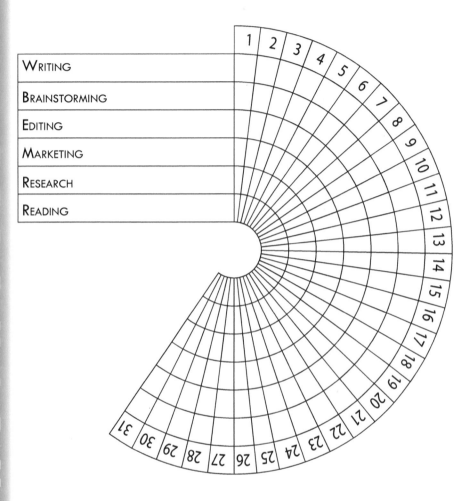

WRITING

BRAINSTORMING

EDITING

MARKETING

RESEARCH

READING

YOUR AVERAGE WORD COUNT FOR THE MONTH

Total Word Count:_____ Divided by _____ days =_____

TOTAL FOR THE YEAR SO FAR

Word Count:_____   Marketing Hours:_____
Brainstorming Hours:_____   Research Hours:_____
Editing Hours:_____   Reading Hours:_____

Journal

What was your **top week**?

_____

What made your **top week** successful?

_____

What was your biggest **obstacle**?

_____

How did you **overcome** this? Or could do better next time?

_____

_____

What was your biggest **achievement**?

_____

_____

What **inspired** you most this month?

_____

Did you **discover** a new writing tip or advice this month?

_____

_____

TOTAL FOR THE MONTH

Word Count:_____   Research Hours:_____
Brainstorming Hours:_____   Reading Hours:_____
Editing Hours:_____
Marketing Hours:_____

TOTAL FOR THE YEAR SO FAR

Word Count:_____   Research Hours:_____
Brainstorming Hours:_____   Reading Hours:_____
Editing Hours:_____
Marketing Hours:_____

Don't forget to color in your grid!

FEBRUARY

MARCH

Now is the time to establish your luck for this month. If you do not see a rainbow, create it. You decide on your version of the pot of gold, but be sure to set your goals so that you can succeed. Don't forget that you can join the 4HP Accountable Authors group on Facebook and find people just like you to collaborate with. Good luck, Fellow Author!

Women's History & Irish American Heritage Month
Mar 2 Ash Wednesday & Read Across America Day

Mar 8 International Day of Women
Mar Daylight Savings Time
Mar 13 The Cheerleader's Birthday

Mar 17 St. Patrick's Day
Mar 19 The Taskmaster's Birthday
Mar 20 March Equinox

WHAT DOES YOUR MONTH LOOK LIKE

Holidays:_____   Weekends:_____

Weekdays:_____   Other:_____

What **project(s)** do you plan on working on?

_____

What **goal** are you aiming to achieve?

_____

What will be your biggest **obstacle** this month?

_____

How will you **overcome** this? Or adjust for this?

_____

What will be your End of the Month **reward**?

_____

GOALS FOR THIS MONTH

Word Count:_____   Marketing Hours:_____

Brainstorming Hours:_____   Research Hours:_____

Editing Hours:_____   Reading Hours:_____

MARCH

DAILY ACCOMPLISHMENTS   **TUESDAY 1**

WORD COUNT:_____   MARKETING HOURS:_____
BRAINSTORMING HOURS:_____   RESEARCH HOURS:_____
EDITING HOURS:_____   READING HOURS:_____

DAILY ACCOMPLISHMENTS   **WEDNESDAY 2**

WORD COUNT:_____   MARKETING HOURS:_____
BRAINSTORMING HOURS:_____   RESEARCH HOURS:_____
EDITING HOURS:_____   READING HOURS:_____

DAILY ACCOMPLISHMENTS   **THURSDAY 3**

WORD COUNT:_____   MARKETING HOURS:_____
BRAINSTORMING HOURS:_____   RESEARCH HOURS:_____
EDITING HOURS:_____   READING HOURS:_____

DAILY ACCOMPLISHMENTS   **FRIDAY 4**

WORD COUNT:_____   MARKETING HOURS:_____
BRAINSTORMING HOURS:_____   RESEARCH HOURS:_____
EDITING HOURS:_____   READING HOURS:_____

DAILY ACCOMPLISHMENTS   **SATURDAY 5**

WORD COUNT:_____   MARKETING HOURS:_____
BRAINSTORMING HOURS:_____   RESEARCH HOURS:_____
EDITING HOURS:_____   READING HOURS:_____

DAILY ACCOMPLISHMENTS   **SUNDAY 6**

WORD COUNT:_____   MARKETING HOURS:_____
BRAINSTORMING HOURS:_____   RESEARCH HOURS:_____
EDITING HOURS:_____   READING HOURS:_____

DAILY ACCOMPLISHMENTS   **MONDAY 7**

WORD COUNT:_____   MARKETING HOURS:_____
BRAINSTORMING HOURS:_____   RESEARCH HOURS:_____
EDITING HOURS:_____   READING HOURS:_____

MARCH

WEEKLY OVERVIEW

EXERCISE: Take 5-minutes to write something with the 2 words below:

Inspire   Queen

Post your exercise on the 4HP Accountable Authors Group on Facebook!

What was your sprint time and top word count?

_____

List a new song you discovered this week:

_____

Favorite food or drink this week:

_____

How did you reward yourself?

_____

What project(s) did you work on?

_____

What are you reading?

_____

What went well this week?

_____

What could improve this week?

_____

_____

_____

TOTAL FOR THE WEEK

Word Count:_____   Marketing Hours:_____
Brainstorming Hours:_____   Research Hours:_____
Editing Hours:_____   Reading Hours:_____

Don't forget to color in your grid!

The Cheerleader

"Writing a novel is like driving a car at night. You can only see as far as your headlights, but you can make the whole trip that way."

~ E. L. Doctorow

THE ARCHITECT

Doing sprints for 10, 20, or 30 minutes at a time will keep your writing at a good pace. Take a moment and try each out! Record your word count and figure out which is the sweet spot. Did you do better sprinting three rounds of 10 minutes with a 5 minute break between or two rounds of 30 minutes with a 10 minute break? Try a few ways and establish a routine.

THE RESEARCHER

For over 50 years Cormac McCarthy wrote on the same typewriter. When it broke, it sold for over $250,000 in 2009 to raise proceeds for the Santa Fe Institute! WOW! I wonder if I could donate that old Windows XP Hewlett Packard in my closet...

THE TASKMASTER

Sit your butt in a chair and write! For the record, this isn't a request. Just do it.

MARCH

DAILY ACCOMPLISHMENTS   **TUESDAY 8**

*Word Count:*_____   *Marketing Hours:*_____
*Brainstorming Hours:*_____   *Research Hours:*_____
*Editing Hours:*_____   *Reading Hours:*_____

DAILY ACCOMPLISHMENTS   **WEDNESDAY 9**

*Word Count:*_____   *Marketing Hours:*_____
*Brainstorming Hours:*_____   *Research Hours:*_____
*Editing Hours:*_____   *Reading Hours:*_____

DAILY ACCOMPLISHMENTS   **THURSDAY 10**

*Word Count:*_____   *Marketing Hours:*_____
*Brainstorming Hours:*_____   *Research Hours:*_____
*Editing Hours:*_____   *Reading Hours:*_____

DAILY ACCOMPLISHMENTS   **FRIDAY 11**

*Word Count:*_____   *Marketing Hours:*_____
*Brainstorming Hours:*_____   *Research Hours:*_____
*Editing Hours:*_____   *Reading Hours:*_____

DAILY ACCOMPLISHMENTS   **SATURDAY 12**

*Word Count:*_____   *Marketing Hours:*_____
*Brainstorming Hours:*_____   *Research Hours:*_____
*Editing Hours:*_____   *Reading Hours:*_____

DAILY ACCOMPLISHMENTS   **SUNDAY 13**

*Word Count:*_____   *Marketing Hours:*_____
*Brainstorming Hours:*_____   *Research Hours:*_____
*Editing Hours:*_____   *Reading Hours:*_____

DAILY ACCOMPLISHMENTS   **MONDAY 14**

*Word Count:*_____   *Marketing Hours:*_____
*Brainstorming Hours:*_____   *Research Hours:*_____
*Editing Hours:*_____   *Reading Hours:*_____

MARCH

WEEKLY OVERVIEW

EXERCISE: Take 5-minutes to write something with the 2 words below:

Pipe   Tea

Post your exercise on the 4HP Accountable Authors Group on Facebook!

What was your sprint time and top word count?

_____

List a new song you discovered this week:

_____

Favorite food or drink this week:

_____

How did you reward yourself?

_____

What project(s) did you work on?

_____

What are you reading?

_____

What went well this week?

_____

What could improve this week?

_____

_____

_____

TOTAL FOR THE WEEK

Word Count:_____ Marketing Hours:_____
Brainstorming Hours:_____ Research Hours:_____
Editing Hours:_____ Reading Hours:_____

Don't forget to color in your grid!

MARCH

The Cheerleader

Art time: Draw a map for your project. It can be a town, a city, a galaxy, a river system, an underground web of tunnels, or a map to buried treasure-- whatever works for you!

THE ARCHITECT

Keep it Active: Add a phrase after your sentence such as "by bunnies." (The car was driven into the field by bunnies.) If it makes sense, the sentence is passive. Consider revising to be more active. (The bunnies drove the car into the field.) When bunnies (or kitties or zombies) don't make sense, you've got it!

MARCH

THE RESEARCHER

*"Too many of us are not living
our dreams because we are
living our fears."*

~ *Les Brown*

THE TASKMASTER

Have you written a review
for the last book you read?
If not, do that now.

MARCH

DAILY ACCOMPLISHMENTS   **TUESDAY 15**

*WORD COUNT:*_____   *MARKETING HOURS:*_____
*BRAINSTORMING HOURS:*_____   *RESEARCH HOURS:*_____
*EDITING HOURS:*_____   *READING HOURS:*_____

DAILY ACCOMPLISHMENTS   **WEDNESDAY 16**

*WORD COUNT:*_____   *MARKETING HOURS:*_____
*BRAINSTORMING HOURS:*_____   *RESEARCH HOURS:*_____
*EDITING HOURS:*_____   *READING HOURS:*_____

DAILY ACCOMPLISHMENTS   **THURSDAY 17**

*WORD COUNT:*_____   *MARKETING HOURS:*_____
*BRAINSTORMING HOURS:*_____   *RESEARCH HOURS:*_____
*EDITING HOURS:*_____   *READING HOURS:*_____

DAILY ACCOMPLISHMENTS   **FRIDAY 18**

*WORD COUNT:*_____   *MARKETING HOURS:*_____
*BRAINSTORMING HOURS:*_____   *RESEARCH HOURS:*_____
*EDITING HOURS:*_____   *READING HOURS:*_____

DAILY ACCOMPLISHMENTS   **SATURDAY 19**

*WORD COUNT:*_____   *MARKETING HOURS:*_____
*BRAINSTORMING HOURS:*_____   *RESEARCH HOURS:*_____
*EDITING HOURS:*_____   *READING HOURS:*_____

DAILY ACCOMPLISHMENTS   **SUNDAY 20**

*WORD COUNT:*_____   *MARKETING HOURS:*_____
*BRAINSTORMING HOURS:*_____   *RESEARCH HOURS:*_____
*EDITING HOURS:*_____   *READING HOURS:*_____

DAILY ACCOMPLISHMENTS   **MONDAY 21**

*WORD COUNT:*_____   *MARKETING HOURS:*_____
*BRAINSTORMING HOURS:*_____   *RESEARCH HOURS:*_____
*EDITING HOURS:*_____   *READING HOURS:*_____

MARCH

WEEKLY OVERVIEW

EXERCISE: Take 5-minutes to write something with the 2 words below:

Herbs   Swing

Post your exercise on the 4HP Accountable Authors Group on Facebook!

What was your sprint time and top word count?

_____

List a new song you discovered this week:

_____

Favorite food or drink this week:

_____

How did you reward yourself?

_____

What project(s) did you work on?

_____

What are you reading?

_____

What went well this week?

_____

What could improve this week?

_____

_____

_____

TOTAL FOR THE WEEK

Word Count:_____   Marketing Hours:_____
Brainstorming Hours:_____   Research Hours:_____
Editing Hours:_____   Reading Hours:_____

Don't forget to color in your grid!

The Cheerleader

Take a moment to do some self-care and changing up your surroundings. Every so often its good to clean up your work station, splurge to buy a new keyboard or pen, and rearrange your area for a fresh vibe to bring it back to life!

THE ARCHITECT

Follow two other writers on social media who are writing in the same genre! If they can make it happen, so can you!

MARCH

THE RESEARCHER

Sometimes we need a writing buddy or trinket! Some of us have pets that fill that void and add them as part of our writing ritual. Lord Byron traveled with dozens of animals which included ten horses, three monkeys, three peacocks, eight dogs, five cats, one crane, one falcon, one eagle, and one crow.

THE TASKMASTER

Pitch your book in 30 seconds or less. Say it out loud. Can you do it? If not, practice in front of a mirror or to another person. It's important to memorize the elevator pitch.

MARCH

DAILY ACCOMPLISHMENTS   **TUESDAY 22**

WORD COUNT:_____   MARKETING HOURS:_____
BRAINSTORMING HOURS:_____   RESEARCH HOURS:_____
EDITING HOURS:_____   READING HOURS:_____

DAILY ACCOMPLISHMENTS   **WEDNESDAY 23**

WORD COUNT:_____   MARKETING HOURS:_____
BRAINSTORMING HOURS:_____   RESEARCH HOURS:_____
EDITING HOURS:_____   READING HOURS:_____

DAILY ACCOMPLISHMENTS   **THURSDAY 24**

WORD COUNT:_____   MARKETING HOURS:_____
BRAINSTORMING HOURS:_____   RESEARCH HOURS:_____
EDITING HOURS:_____   READING HOURS:_____

DAILY ACCOMPLISHMENTS   **FRIDAY 25**

WORD COUNT:_____   MARKETING HOURS:_____
BRAINSTORMING HOURS:_____   RESEARCH HOURS:_____
EDITING HOURS:_____   READING HOURS:_____

DAILY ACCOMPLISHMENTS   **SATURDAY 26**

WORD COUNT:_____   MARKETING HOURS:_____
BRAINSTORMING HOURS:_____   RESEARCH HOURS:_____
EDITING HOURS:_____   READING HOURS:_____

DAILY ACCOMPLISHMENTS   **SUNDAY 27**

WORD COUNT:_____   MARKETING HOURS:_____
BRAINSTORMING HOURS:_____   RESEARCH HOURS:_____
EDITING HOURS:_____   READING HOURS:_____

DAILY ACCOMPLISHMENTS   **MONDAY 28**

WORD COUNT:_____   MARKETING HOURS:_____
BRAINSTORMING HOURS:_____   RESEARCH HOURS:_____
EDITING HOURS:_____   READING HOURS:_____

MARCH

WEEKLY OVERVIEW

EXERCISE: Take 5-minutes to write something with the 2 words below:

Pursue   **Duck**

Post your exercise on the 4HP Accountable Authors Group on Facebook!

What was your sprint time and top word count?

_____

List a new song you discovered this week:

_____

Favorite food or drink this week:

_____

How did you reward yourself?

_____

What project(s) did you work on?

_____

What are you reading?

_____

What went well this week?

_____

What could improve this week?

_____

_____

_____

TOTAL FOR THE WEEK

Word Count:_____   Marketing Hours:_____
Brainstorming Hours:_____   Research Hours:_____
Editing Hours:_____   Reading Hours:_____

Don't forget to color in your grid!

MARCH

MARCH

The Cheerleader

"I have been successful probably because I have always realized that I knew nothing about writing and have merely tried to tell an interesting story entertainingly."

~ Edgar Rice Burroughs

THE ARCHITECT

Weave subtext throughout your writing. This will give your story a layered, nuanced message that isn't shoved into the reader's face.

THE RESEARCHER

Take two characters who are inseparable and reveal something that will shake their relationship. A great example is when Harry Houdini stopped being besties with Sir Arthur Conan Doyle when he revealed he was a spiritualist and believed Houdini performed real magic!

THE TASKMASTER

You can be your worst critic (enemy). STOP IT!!! You're awesome. I believe in you.

MARCH

DAILY ACCOMPLISHMENTS **TUESDAY 29**

WORD COUNT:_____ MARKETING HOURS:_____
BRAINSTORMING HOURS:_____ RESEARCH HOURS:_____
EDITING HOURS:_____ READING HOURS:_____

DAILY ACCOMPLISHMENTS **WEDNESDAY 30**

WORD COUNT:_____ MARKETING HOURS:_____
BRAINSTORMING HOURS:_____ RESEARCH HOURS:_____
EDITING HOURS:_____ READING HOURS:_____

DAILY ACCOMPLISHMENTS **THURSDAY 31**

WORD COUNT:_____ MARKETING HOURS:_____
BRAINSTORMING HOURS:_____ RESEARCH HOURS:_____
EDITING HOURS:_____ READING HOURS:_____

The Cheerleader

"Perfectionism is the voice of the oppressor, the enemy of the people. It will keep you cramped and insane your whole life, and it is the main obstacle between you and a shitty first draft. I think perfectionism is based on the obsessive belief that if you run carefully enough, hitting each stepping-stone just right, you won't have to die. The truth is that you will die anyway and that a lot of people who aren't even looking at their feet are going to do a whole lot better than you, and have a lot more fun while they're doing it."

-Anne Lamott (Bird by Bird: Some Instructions on Writing and Life)

WEEKLY OVERVIEW

EXERCISE: Take 5-minutes to write something with the 2 words below:

Scold   Tawdry

Post your exercise on the 4HP Accountable Authors Group on Facebook!

What was your sprint time and top word count?

_____

List a new song you discovered this week:

_____

Favorite food or drink this week:

_____

How did you reward yourself?

_____

What project(s) did you work on?

_____

What are you reading?

_____

What went well this week?

_____

What could improve this week?

_____

_____

_____

TOTAL FOR THE WEEK

Word Count:_____   Marketing Hours:_____
Brainstorming Hours:_____   Research Hours:_____
Editing Hours:_____   Reading Hours:_____

Don't forget to color in your grid!

Monthly Activity Grid

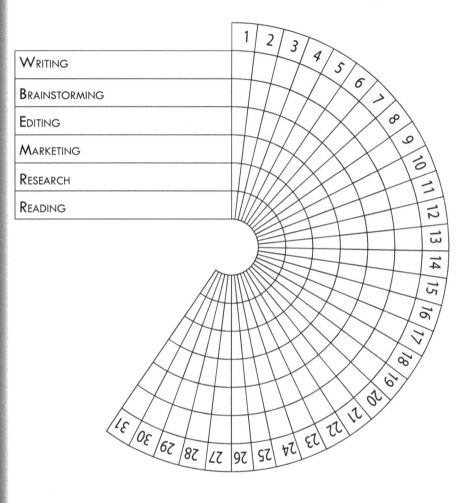

M A R C H

WRITING

BRAINSTORMING

EDITING

MARKETING

RESEARCH

READING

YOUR AVERAGE WORD COUNT FOR THE MONTH

Total Word Count:_____ Divided by _____ days =_____

TOTAL FOR THE YEAR SO FAR

Word Count:_____   Marketing Hours:_____
Brainstorming Hours:_____   Research Hours:_____
Editing Hours:_____   Reading Hours:_____

JOURNAL

MARCH

What was your **top week**?

_____

What made your **top week** successful?

_____

What was your biggest **obstacle**?

_____

How did you **overcome** this? Or could do better next time?

_____

_____

What was your biggest **achievement**?

_____

_____

What **inspired** you most this month?

_____

Did you **discover** a new writing tip or advice this month?

_____

_____

TOTAL FOR THE MONTH

Word Count:_____   Research Hours:_____
Brainstorming Hours:_____   Reading Hours:_____
Editing Hours:_____
Marketing Hours:_____

TOTAL FOR THE YEAR SO FAR

Word Count:_____   Research Hours:_____
Brainstorming Hours:_____   Reading Hours:_____
Editing Hours:_____
Marketing Hours:_____

Don't forget to color in your grid!

APRIL

April is a month of new beginings. Spring is in full swing, and new animals emerge into the world. Make sure you take some time to step outside and see the world blooming around you. Who knows who or what you might encounter outside your door?

Apr 1 April Fool's Day
Apr 12 National Library Workers's Day
Apr 15 Good Friday

Apr 17 Easter Sunday
Apr 21 World Creativity and Innovation Day
Apr 22 Earth Day

Apr 23 World Book and Copyright Day & English Language Day,

WHAT DOES YOUR MONTH LOOK LIKE

Holidays:_____   Weekends:_____
Weekdays:_____   Other:_____

What **project(s)** do you plan on working on?

_____

What **goal** are you aiming to achieve?

_____

What will be your biggest **obstacle** this month?

_____

How will you **overcome** this? Or adjust for this?

_____

What will be your End of the Month **reward**?

_____

GOALS FOR THIS MONTH

Word Count:_____   Marketing Hours:_____
Brainstorming Hours:_____   Research Hours:_____
Editing Hours:_____   Reading Hours:_____

APRIL

Week 1

Daily Accomplishments   Friday 1

Word Count:_____   Marketing Hours:_____
Brainstorming Hours:_____   Research Hours:_____
Editing Hours:_____   Reading Hours:_____

Daily Accomplishments   Saturday 2

Word Count:_____   Marketing Hours:_____
Brainstorming Hours:_____   Research Hours:_____
Editing Hours:_____   Reading Hours:_____

Daily Accomplishments   Sunday 3

Word Count:_____   Marketing Hours:_____
Brainstorming Hours:_____   Research Hours:_____
Editing Hours:_____   Reading Hours:_____

Daily Accomplishments   Monday 4

Word Count:_____   Marketing Hours:_____
Brainstorming Hours:_____   Research Hours:_____
Editing Hours:_____   Reading Hours:_____

Daily Accomplishments   Tuesday 5

Word Count:_____   Marketing Hours:_____
Brainstorming Hours:_____   Research Hours:_____
Editing Hours:_____   Reading Hours:_____

Daily Accomplishments   Wednesday 6

Word Count:_____   Marketing Hours:_____
Brainstorming Hours:_____   Research Hours:_____
Editing Hours:_____   Reading Hours:_____

Daily Accomplishments   Thursday 7

Word Count:_____   Marketing Hours:_____
Brainstorming Hours:_____   Research Hours:_____
Editing Hours:_____   Reading Hours:_____

WEEKLY OVERVIEW

EXERCISE: Take 5-minutes to write something with the 2 words below:

Pasta   Computer

Post your exercise on the 4HP Accountable Authors Group on Facebook!

What was your sprint time and top word count?

_____

List a new song you discovered this week:

_____

Favorite food or drink this week:

_____

How did you reward yourself?

_____

What project(s) did you work on?

_____

What are you reading?

_____

What went well this week?

_____

What could improve this week?

_____

_____

_____

TOTAL FOR THE WEEK

Word Count:_____   Marketing Hours:_____
Brainstorming Hours:_____   Research Hours:_____
Editing Hours:_____   Reading Hours:_____

Don't forget to color in your grid!

The Cheerleader

A spoonful of sugar helps the medicine go down. Record one sweet thing that offsets one negative thing this week.

THE ARCHITECT

Five Minute Break Time: Stand up. Walk around. Go outside if you can. Look skyward, study a different wall, check out a new space. Set a timer, then return to writing when it goes off.

THE RESEARCHER

Russian writer Boris Pasternak refused the Nobel Prize for Literature for *Doctor Zhivago* in 1958. Why? He feared the Soviet government would arrest him or his family! So, what's keeping you from reaching higher?

THE TASKMASTER

"You don't have to be great to start, but you have to start to be great."

~ *Zig Ziglar*

Are you maintaining your monthly goals? You're in control of that. Treat this with the same passion you want your readers to feel about your work.

APRIL

WEEK 2

DAILY ACCOMPLISHMENTS	**FRIDAY 8**
WORD COUNT:	*MARKETING HOURS:*
BRAINSTORMING HOURS:	*RESEARCH HOURS:*
EDITING HOURS:	*READING HOURS:*

DAILY ACCOMPLISHMENTS	**SATURDAY 9**
WORD COUNT:	*MARKETING HOURS:*
BRAINSTORMING HOURS:	*RESEARCH HOURS:*
EDITING HOURS:	*READING HOURS:*

DAILY ACCOMPLISHMENTS	**SUNDAY 10**
WORD COUNT:	*MARKETING HOURS:*
BRAINSTORMING HOURS:	*RESEARCH HOURS:*
EDITING HOURS:	*READING HOURS:*

DAILY ACCOMPLISHMENTS	**MONDAY 11**
WORD COUNT:	*MARKETING HOURS:*
BRAINSTORMING HOURS:	*RESEARCH HOURS:*
EDITING HOURS:	*READING HOURS:*

DAILY ACCOMPLISHMENTS	**TUESDAY 12**
WORD COUNT:	*MARKETING HOURS:*
BRAINSTORMING HOURS:	*RESEARCH HOURS:*
EDITING HOURS:	*READING HOURS:*

DAILY ACCOMPLISHMENTS	**WEDNESDAY 13**
WORD COUNT:	*MARKETING HOURS:*
BRAINSTORMING HOURS:	*RESEARCH HOURS:*
EDITING HOURS:	*READING HOURS:*

DAILY ACCOMPLISHMENTS	**THURSDAY 14**
WORD COUNT:	*MARKETING HOURS:*
BRAINSTORMING HOURS:	*RESEARCH HOURS:*
EDITING HOURS:	*READING HOURS:*

Weekly Overview

Alluring   Attic

Post your exercise on the 4HP Accountable Authors Group on Facebook!

What was your sprint time and top word count?

_____

List a new song you discovered this week:

_____

Favorite food or drink this week:

_____

How did you reward yourself?

_____

What project(s) did you work on?

_____

What are you reading?

_____

What went well this week?

_____

What could improve this week?

_____

_____

_____

Total for the Week

Word Count:_____   Marketing Hours:_____
Brainstorming Hours:_____   Research Hours:_____
Editing Hours:_____   Reading Hours:_____

Don't forget to color in your grid!

APRIL

The Cheerleader

Find something that "Sparks Joy" and keep it within sight of your writing space. Sometimes you need a gentle reminder to stay positive.

THE ARCHITECT

Sensory Overload: Describe your surroundings by using all five senses.

THE RESEARCHER

"Everybody walks past a thousand story ideas every day. The good writers are the ones who see five or six of them. Most people don't see any."

~ Orson Scott Card

THE TASKMASTER

Pick up or discover a new book on writing. Find stronger word choices, master character dialogue, or add depth to worldbuilding and plot.

APRIL

APRIL

DAILY ACCOMPLISHMENTS   FRIDAY 15

WORD COUNT:_____   MARKETING HOURS:_____
BRAINSTORMING HOURS:_____   RESEARCH HOURS:_____
EDITING HOURS:_____   READING HOURS:_____

DAILY ACCOMPLISHMENTS   SATURDAY 16

WORD COUNT:_____   MARKETING HOURS:_____
BRAINSTORMING HOURS:_____   RESEARCH HOURS:_____
EDITING HOURS:_____   READING HOURS:_____

DAILY ACCOMPLISHMENTS   SUNDAY 17

WORD COUNT:_____   MARKETING HOURS:_____
BRAINSTORMING HOURS:_____   RESEARCH HOURS:_____
EDITING HOURS:_____   READING HOURS:_____

DAILY ACCOMPLISHMENTS   MONDAY 18

WORD COUNT:_____   MARKETING HOURS:_____
BRAINSTORMING HOURS:_____   RESEARCH HOURS:_____
EDITING HOURS:_____   READING HOURS:_____

DAILY ACCOMPLISHMENTS   TUESDAY 19

WORD COUNT:_____   MARKETING HOURS:_____
BRAINSTORMING HOURS:_____   RESEARCH HOURS:_____
EDITING HOURS:_____   READING HOURS:_____

DAILY ACCOMPLISHMENTS   WEDNESDAY 20

WORD COUNT:_____   MARKETING HOURS:_____
BRAINSTORMING HOURS:_____   RESEARCH HOURS:_____
EDITING HOURS:_____   READING HOURS:_____

DAILY ACCOMPLISHMENTS   THURSDAY 21

WORD COUNT:_____   MARKETING HOURS:_____
BRAINSTORMING HOURS:_____   RESEARCH HOURS:_____
EDITING HOURS:_____   READING HOURS:_____

EXERCISE: Take 5-minutes to write something with the 2 words below:

Dodge   Fluttering

Post your exercise on the 4HP Accountable Authors Group on Facebook!

What was your sprint time and top word count?

_____

List a new song you discovered this week:

_____

Favorite food or drink this week:

_____

How did you reward yourself?

_____

What project(s) did you work on?

_____

What are you reading?

_____

What went well this week?

_____

What could improve this week?

_____

_____

_____

TOTAL FOR THE WEEK

Word Count:_____   Marketing Hours:_____
Brainstorming Hours:_____   Research Hours:_____
Editing Hours:_____   Reading Hours:_____

Don't forget to color in your grid!

APRIL

The Cheerleader

"You don't actually have to write anything until you've thought it out. This is an enormous relief, and you can sit there searching for the point at which the story becomes a toboggan and starts to slide."

~ Marie de Nervaud

APRIL

THE ARCHITECT

Time to Ctrl F your overused words. List the troublesome words here that keep sneaking back in.

THE RESEARCHER

Some of us like to write about immortal beings and vampires that are born in obscure times and dates. Remember even a mere mortal may not know the date of their birthday. Canadian-American author Saul Bellow knew his parents arrived in Quebec in 1915 when he was born, but his parents couldn't remember if it was June or July or neither. Worse, the city hall with his records had burned down, a common occurence worldwide

THE TASKMASTER

How do you track your ideas? A journal's a great way to ensure you never lose a story idea. You can also use notes in your phone or voice memos. Never lose the awesomeness your imagination is generating.

APRIL

DAILY ACCOMPLISHMENTS   **FRIDAY 22**

WORD COUNT:_____   MARKETING HOURS:_____
BRAINSTORMING HOURS:_____ RESEARCH HOURS:_____
EDITING HOURS:_____   READING HOURS:_____

DAILY ACCOMPLISHMENTS   **SATURDAY 23**

WORD COUNT:_____   MARKETING HOURS:_____
BRAINSTORMING HOURS:_____ RESEARCH HOURS:_____
EDITING HOURS:_____   READING HOURS:_____

DAILY ACCOMPLISHMENTS   **SUNDAY 24**

WORD COUNT:_____   MARKETING HOURS:_____
BRAINSTORMING HOURS:_____ RESEARCH HOURS:_____
EDITING HOURS:_____   READING HOURS:_____

DAILY ACCOMPLISHMENTS   **MONDAY 25**

WORD COUNT:_____   MARKETING HOURS:_____
BRAINSTORMING HOURS:_____ RESEARCH HOURS:_____
EDITING HOURS:_____   READING HOURS:_____

DAILY ACCOMPLISHMENTS   **TUESDAY 26**

WORD COUNT:_____   MARKETING HOURS:_____
BRAINSTORMING HOURS:_____ RESEARCH HOURS:_____
EDITING HOURS:_____   READING HOURS:_____

DAILY ACCOMPLISHMENTS   **WEDNESDAY 27**

WORD COUNT:_____   MARKETING HOURS:_____
BRAINSTORMING HOURS:_____ RESEARCH HOURS:_____
EDITING HOURS:_____   READING HOURS:_____

DAILY ACCOMPLISHMENTS   **THURSDAY 28**

WORD COUNT:_____   MARKETING HOURS:_____
BRAINSTORMING HOURS:_____ RESEARCH HOURS:_____
EDITING HOURS:_____   READING HOURS:_____

APRIL

WEEKLY OVERVIEW

EXERCISE: Take 5-minutes to write something with the 2 words below:

Gondola   Hoodwink

Post your exercise on the 4HP Accountable Authors Group on Facebook!

What was your sprint time and top word count?

_____

List a new song you discovered this week:

_____

Favorite food or drink this week:

_____

How did you reward yourself?

_____

What project(s) did you work on?

_____

What are you reading?

_____

What went well this week?

_____

What could improve this week?

_____

_____

_____

TOTAL FOR THE WEEK

Word Count:_____   Marketing Hours:_____
Brainstorming Hours:_____   Research Hours:_____
Editing Hours:_____   Reading Hours:_____

Don't forget to color in your grid!

APRIL

The Cheerleader

What is your favorite way to write? Sometimes listening to music from the time or place you're writing about will get you into

THE ARCHITECT

"If something isn't working, if you have a story that you've built and it's blocked and you can't figure it out, take your favorite scene, or your very best idea or set-piece, and cut it. It's brutal, but sometimes inevitable."

~ Joss Whedon

THE RESEARCHER

What would make your character pass out? And if it did, how would that affect the plot and world? For example, French novelist Stendhal passed out after seeing the Basilica of Santa Croce in Florence. Now we call fainting when viewing exquisite art Stendhal Syndrome!

THE TASKMASTER

Spring Cleaning: Set a timer for seven minutes. Write down every project idea in your brain until the alarm rings. Get those thoughts on paper (for later use on a future project). Do this as many times as needed to not interphere with your current project.

APRIL

APRIL

DAILY ACCOMPLISHMENTS	FRIDAY 29
WORD COUNT:_____	MARKETING HOURS:_____
BRAINSTORMING HOURS:_____	RESEARCH HOURS:_____
EDITING HOURS:_____	READING HOURS:_____

DAILY ACCOMPLISHMENTS	SATURDAY 30
WORD COUNT:_____	MARKETING HOURS:_____
BRAINSTORMING HOURS:_____	RESEARCH HOURS:_____
EDITING HOURS:_____	READING HOURS:_____

THE ARCHITECT

Find a podcast about authors, writing, even book reviews on books similar to your own. Get to know your fellow authors! (*We recommend Drinking with Authors*).

Listen to it as you go outside for a walk. Exercise is important. Self-care has to be part of your day-to-day routine. Learning more about writing is important too!

EXERCISE: Take 5-minutes to write something with the 2 words below:

Exotic   Garlic

Post your exercise on the 4HP Accountable Authors Group on Facebook!

What was your sprint time and top word count?

_____

List a new song you discovered this week:

_____

Favorite food or drink this week:

_____

How did you reward yourself?

_____

What project(s) did you work on?

_____

What are you reading?

_____

What went well this week?

_____

What could improve this week?

_____

_____

_____

TOTAL FOR THE WEEK

Word Count:_____   Marketing Hours:_____
Brainstorming Hours:_____   Research Hours:_____
Editing Hours:_____   Reading Hours:_____

Don't forget to color in your grid!

MONTHLY ACTIVITY GRID

APRIL

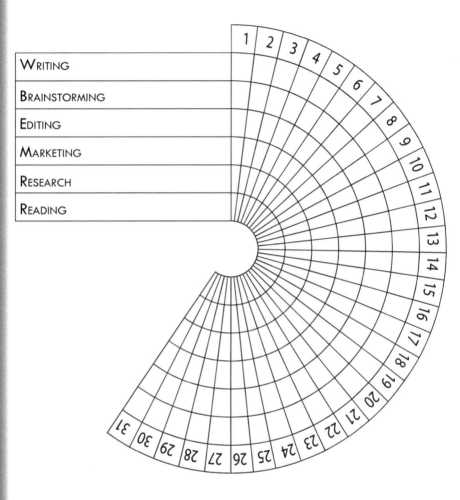

WRITING

BRAINSTORMING

EDITING

MARKETING

RESEARCH

READING

YOUR AVERAGE WORD COUNT FOR THE MONTH

Total Word Count:_____ Divided by _____ days =_____

TOTAL FOR THE YEAR SO FAR

Word Count:_____   Marketing Hours:_____
Brainstorming Hours:_____   Research Hours:_____
Editing Hours:_____   Reading Hours:_____

JOURNAL

What was your **top week**?

_____

What made your **top week** successful?

_____

What was your biggest **obstacle**?

_____

How did you **overcome** this? Or could do better next time?

_____

_____

What was your biggest **achievement**?

_____

_____

What **inspired** you most this month?

_____

Did you **discover** a new writing tip or advice this month?

_____

_____

TOTAL FOR THE MONTH

Word Count:_____   Research Hours:_____
Brainstorming Hours:_____   Reading Hours:_____
Editing Hours:_____
Marketing Hours:_____

TOTAL FOR THE YEAR SO FAR

Word Count:_____   Research Hours:_____
Brainstorming Hours:_____   Reading Hours:_____
Editing Hours:_____
Marketing Hours:_____

Don't forget to color in your grid!

APRIL

MAY

The school year may almost be over. You might have to attend a graduation or be graduating yourself. Do not let that slow you down. Maybe grab your laptop, go write outside, and enjoy all that nature around you inspires.

Asian Pacific American Heritage & Jewish American Heritage Month

May 5 Cinco de Mayo
May 8 Mother's Day
May 13 Friday the 13th

May 21
International Tea Day
May 30 Memorial Day

WHAT DOES YOUR MONTH LOOK LIKE

Holidays:_____   Weekends:_____
Weekdays:_____   Other:_____

What **project(s)** do you plan on working on?

_____

What **goal** are you aiming to achieve?

_____

What will be your biggest **obstacle** this month?

_____

How will you **overcome** this? Or adjust for this?

_____

What will be your End of the Month **reward**?

_____

GOALS FOR THIS MONTH

Word Count:_____   Marketing Hours:_____
Brainstorming Hours:_____   Research Hours:_____
Editing Hours:_____   Reading Hours:_____

DAILY ACCOMPLISHMENTS   **SUNDAY 1**

WORD COUNT: _____   *MARKETING HOURS:* _____
BRAINSTORMING HOURS: _____ *RESEARCH HOURS:* _____
EDITING HOURS: _____   *READING HOURS:* _____

DAILY ACCOMPLISHMENTS   **MONDAY 2**

WORD COUNT: _____   *MARKETING HOURS:* _____
BRAINSTORMING HOURS: _____ *RESEARCH HOURS:* _____
EDITING HOURS: _____   *READING HOURS:* _____

DAILY ACCOMPLISHMENTS   **TUESDAY 3**

WORD COUNT: _____   *MARKETING HOURS:* _____
BRAINSTORMING HOURS: _____ *RESEARCH HOURS:* _____
EDITING HOURS: _____   *READING HOURS:* _____

DAILY ACCOMPLISHMENTS   **WEDNESDAY 4**

WORD COUNT: _____   *MARKETING HOURS:* _____
BRAINSTORMING HOURS: _____ *RESEARCH HOURS:* _____
EDITING HOURS: _____   *READING HOURS:* _____

DAILY ACCOMPLISHMENTS   **THURSDAY 5**

WORD COUNT: _____   *MARKETING HOURS:* _____
BRAINSTORMING HOURS: _____ *RESEARCH HOURS:* _____
EDITING HOURS: _____   *READING HOURS:* _____

DAILY ACCOMPLISHMENTS   **FRIDAY 6**

WORD COUNT: _____   *MARKETING HOURS:* _____
BRAINSTORMING HOURS: _____ *RESEARCH HOURS:* _____
EDITING HOURS: _____   *READING HOURS:* _____

DAILY ACCOMPLISHMENTS   **SATURDAY 7**

WORD COUNT: _____   *MARKETING HOURS:* _____
BRAINSTORMING HOURS: _____ *RESEARCH HOURS:* _____
EDITING HOURS: _____   *READING HOURS:* _____

MAY

WEEKLY OVERVIEW

EXERCISE: Take 5-minutes to write something with the 2 words below:

Frustrate   Tower

Post your exercise on the 4HP Accountable Authors Group on Facebook!

What was your sprint time and top word count?

_____

List a new song you discovered this week:

_____

Favorite food or drink this week:

_____

How did you reward yourself?

_____

What project(s) did you work on?

_____

What are you reading?

_____

What went well this week?

_____

What could improve this week?

_____

_____

_____

TOTAL FOR THE WEEK

Word Count:_____   Marketing Hours:_____
Brainstorming Hours:_____   Research Hours:_____
Editing Hours:_____   Reading Hours:_____

Don't forget to color in your grid!

The Cheerleader

Art Time: Sketch yourself reaching your year end writing goals. Visualization helps with motivation!

THE ARCHITECT

Eliminate passive voice as much as possible.

Passive: This fantasy novel was written by Vanessa.

Active: Vanessa wrote this fantasy novel.

THE RESEARCHER

Keep getting lost down a Research Rabbit Hole? No worries. Take a moment to make a DO and DON'T Want List, then focus on character, world, or plot.

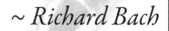

THE TASKMASTER

"A professional writer is an amateur who did not quit."

~ Richard Bach

You are a professional writer. How do I know this? You bought a skill book to keep you organized and on task. Only a professional would do that.

MAY

WEEK 2

DAILY ACCOMPLISHMENTS	**SUNDAY 8**
WORD COUNT:	MARKETING HOURS:
BRAINSTORMING HOURS:	RESEARCH HOURS:
EDITING HOURS:	READING HOURS:

DAILY ACCOMPLISHMENTS	**MONDAY 9**
WORD COUNT:	MARKETING HOURS:
BRAINSTORMING HOURS:	RESEARCH HOURS:
EDITING HOURS:	READING HOURS:

DAILY ACCOMPLISHMENTS	**TUESDAY 10**
WORD COUNT:	MARKETING HOURS:
BRAINSTORMING HOURS:	RESEARCH HOURS:
EDITING HOURS:	READING HOURS:

DAILY ACCOMPLISHMENTS	**WEDNESDAY 11**
WORD COUNT:	MARKETING HOURS:
BRAINSTORMING HOURS:	RESEARCH HOURS:
EDITING HOURS:	READING HOURS:

DAILY ACCOMPLISHMENTS	**THURSDAY 12**
WORD COUNT:	MARKETING HOURS:
BRAINSTORMING HOURS:	RESEARCH HOURS:
EDITING HOURS:	READING HOURS:

DAILY ACCOMPLISHMENTS	**FRIDAY 13**
WORD COUNT:	MARKETING HOURS:
BRAINSTORMING HOURS:	RESEARCH HOURS:
EDITING HOURS:	READING HOURS:

DAILY ACCOMPLISHMENTS	**SATURDAY 14**
WORD COUNT:	MARKETING HOURS:
BRAINSTORMING HOURS:	RESEARCH HOURS:
EDITING HOURS:	READING HOURS:

WEEKLY OVERVIEW

EXERCISE: Take 5-minutes to write something with the 2 words below:

Bulldozer   Monster

Post your exercise on the 4HP Accountable Authors Group on Facebook!

What was your sprint time and top word count?

_____

List a new song you discovered this week:

_____

Favorite food or drink this week:

_____

How did you reward yourself?

_____

What project(s) did you work on?

_____

What are you reading?

_____

What went well this week?

_____

What could improve this week?

_____

_____

_____

TOTAL FOR THE WEEK

Word Count:_____   Marketing Hours:_____
Brainstorming Hours:_____   Research Hours:_____
Editing Hours:_____   Reading Hours:_____

Don't forget to color in your grid!

MAY

The Cheerleader

Pay attention to the things that excite you: music, books, movies, hobbies, etc. Use them as inspiration for your stories.

THE ARCHITECT

The original or the remake-- which is better?

Defend your position.

MAY

THE RESEARCHER

The writer is an explorer. Every step is an advance into a new land.

~ Ralph Waldo Emerson

THE TASKMASTER

You have fans (or will have fans if you haven't been published yet). Even if you can't see them, they're rooting for you--so don't forget to root for yourself!

MAY

DAILY ACCOMPLISHMENTS   **SUNDAY 15**

Word Count:_____   Marketing Hours:_____
Brainstorming Hours:_____   Research Hours:_____
Editing Hours:_____   Reading Hours:_____

DAILY ACCOMPLISHMENTS   **MONDAY 16**

Word Count:_____   Marketing Hours:_____
Brainstorming Hours:_____   Research Hours:_____
Editing Hours:_____   Reading Hours:_____

DAILY ACCOMPLISHMENTS   **TUESDAY 17**

Word Count:_____   Marketing Hours:_____
Brainstorming Hours:_____   Research Hours:_____
Editing Hours:_____   Reading Hours:_____

DAILY ACCOMPLISHMENTS   **WEDNESDAY 18**

Word Count:_____   Marketing Hours:_____
Brainstorming Hours:_____   Research Hours:_____
Editing Hours:_____   Reading Hours:_____

DAILY ACCOMPLISHMENTS   **THURSDAY 19**

Word Count:_____   Marketing Hours:_____
Brainstorming Hours:_____   Research Hours:_____
Editing Hours:_____   Reading Hours:_____

DAILY ACCOMPLISHMENTS   **FRIDAY 20**

Word Count:_____   Marketing Hours:_____
Brainstorming Hours:_____   Research Hours:_____
Editing Hours:_____   Reading Hours:_____

DAILY ACCOMPLISHMENTS   **SATURDAY 21**

Word Count:_____   Marketing Hours:_____
Brainstorming Hours:_____   Research Hours:_____
Editing Hours:_____   Reading Hours:_____

WEEKLY OVERVIEW

EXERCISE: Take 5-minutes to write something with the 2 words below:

Bib   Train

Post your exercise on the 4HP Accountable Authors Group on Facebook!

What was your sprint time and top word count?

_____

List a new song you discovered this week:

_____

Favorite food or drink this week:

_____

How did you reward yourself?

_____

What project(s) did you work on?

_____

What are you reading?

_____

What went well this week?

_____

What could improve this week?

_____

_____

_____

TOTAL FOR THE WEEK

Word Count:_____   Marketing Hours:_____
Brainstorming Hours:_____   Research Hours:_____
Editing Hours:_____   Reading Hours:_____

Don't forget to color in your grid!

MAY

The Cheerleader

Find a book outside of your comfort zone. Give it a try! (Support your local library!)

THE ARCHITECT

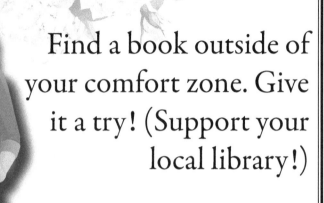

Bio Update: Review your author biography. Tweak for changes.

MAY

THE RESEARCHER

Use multiple sources to find tidbits for your current research topic. Don't trust everything you read on the internet. Try going to a local museum, dive into forums, email a professional, and go outside your normal means!

THE TASKMASTER

Increase your word count for next week regardless of your target. Little jumps help get you there faster.

MAY

WEEK 4

DAILY ACCOMPLISHMENTS	**SUNDAY 22**
WORD COUNT:	MARKETING HOURS:
BRAINSTORMING HOURS:	RESEARCH HOURS:
EDITING HOURS:	READING HOURS:

DAILY ACCOMPLISHMENTS	**MONDAY 23**
WORD COUNT:	MARKETING HOURS:
BRAINSTORMING HOURS:	RESEARCH HOURS:
EDITING HOURS:	READING HOURS:

DAILY ACCOMPLISHMENTS	**TUESDAY 24**
WORD COUNT:	MARKETING HOURS:
BRAINSTORMING HOURS:	RESEARCH HOURS:
EDITING HOURS:	READING HOURS:

DAILY ACCOMPLISHMENTS	**WEDNESDAY 25**
WORD COUNT:	MARKETING HOURS:
BRAINSTORMING HOURS:	RESEARCH HOURS:
EDITING HOURS:	READING HOURS:

DAILY ACCOMPLISHMENTS	**THURSDAY 26**
WORD COUNT:	MARKETING HOURS:
BRAINSTORMING HOURS:	RESEARCH HOURS:
EDITING HOURS:	READING HOURS:

DAILY ACCOMPLISHMENTS	**FRIDAY 27**
WORD COUNT:	MARKETING HOURS:
BRAINSTORMING HOURS:	RESEARCH HOURS:
EDITING HOURS:	READING HOURS:

DAILY ACCOMPLISHMENTS	**SATURDAY 28**
WORD COUNT:	MARKETING HOURS:
BRAINSTORMING HOURS:	RESEARCH HOURS:
EDITING HOURS:	READING HOURS:

EXERCISE: Take 5-minutes to write something with the 2 words below:

Judo   Night

Post your exercise on the 4HP Accountable Authors Group on Facebook!

What was your sprint time and top word count?

_____

List a new song you discovered this week:

_____

Favorite food or drink this week:

_____

How did you reward yourself?

_____

What project(s) did you work on?

_____

What are you reading?

_____

What went well this week?

_____

What could improve this week?

_____

_____

_____

MAY

TOTAL FOR THE WEEK

Word Count:_____   Marketing Hours:_____
Brainstorming Hours:_____   Research Hours:_____
Editing Hours:_____   Reading Hours:_____

Don't forget to color in your grid!

The Cheerleader

"Do not hoard what seems good for a later place in the book, or for another book; give it, give it all, give it now."

~ Annie Dillard

THE ARCHITECT

Wordbuilding is fun because you create all the rules. But don't forget to write them down. Be consistent.

THE RESEARCHER

Quick! List all the signs of being undead (whether your own symptoms or asking for friend)! Are these signs of a vampire bite or zombie infection?

THE TASKMASTER

Are you overediting your work? Stop it. Get the entire story on paper first. Then go back and review what you've done. It's easy to fall into the editing trap. If you need to tag that part with a comment and circle back.

MAY

DAILY ACCOMPLISHMENTS **SUNDAY 29**

WORD COUNT:_____ MARKETING HOURS:_____
BRAINSTORMING HOURS:_____ RESEARCH HOURS:_____
EDITING HOURS:_____ READING HOURS:_____

DAILY ACCOMPLISHMENTS **MONDAY 30**

WORD COUNT:_____ MARKETING HOURS:_____
BRAINSTORMING HOURS:_____ RESEARCH HOURS:_____
EDITING HOURS:_____ READING HOURS:_____

DAILY ACCOMPLISHMENTS **TUESDAY 31**

WORD COUNT:_____ MARKETING HOURS:_____
BRAINSTORMING HOURS:_____ RESEARCH HOURS:_____
EDITING HOURS:_____ READING HOURS:_____

THE TASKMASTER

Now is the time to establish your luck for this month. If you do not see a rainbow, create it. You decide on your version of the pot of gold, but be sure to set your goals so that you can succeed. Don't forget that you can join the 4HP Accountable Authors group on Facebook and find people just like you to collaborate with. Good luck, Fellow Author!

Exercise: Take 5-minutes to write something with the 2 words below:

Exile   Giraffe

Post your exercise on the 4HP Accountable Authors Group on Facebook!

What was your sprint time and top word count?

_____

List a new song you discovered this week:

_____

Favorite food or drink this week:

_____

How did you reward yourself?

_____

What project(s) did you work on?

_____

What are you reading?

_____

What went well this week?

_____

What could improve this week?

_____

_____

_____

Total for the Week

Word Count:_____   Marketing Hours:_____
Brainstorming Hours:_____   Research Hours:_____
Editing Hours:_____   Reading Hours:_____

Don't forget to color in your grid!

Monthly Activity Grid

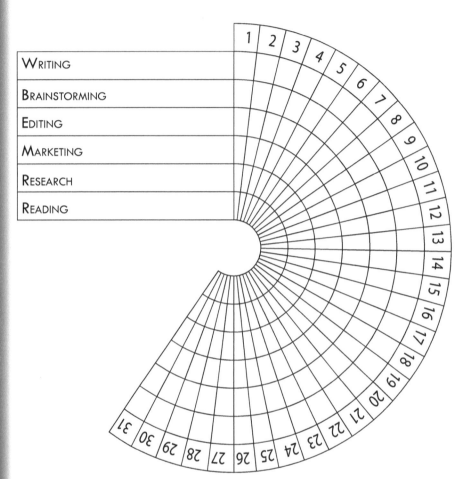

MAY

Writing

Brainstorming

Editing

Marketing

Research

Reading

Your Average Word Count for the Month

Total Word Count:_____ Divided by _____ days =_____

Total for the Year So Far

Word Count:_____   Marketing Hours:_____
Brainstorming Hours:_____   Research Hours:_____
Editing Hours:_____   Reading Hours:_____

JOURNAL

MAY

What was your **top week**?

_____

What made your **top week** successful?

_____

What was your biggest **obstacle**?

_____

How did you **overcome** this? Or could do better next time?

_____

_____

What was your biggest **achievement**?

_____

_____

What **inspired** you most this month?

_____

Did you **discover** a new writing tip or advice this month?

_____

_____

_____

TOTAL FOR THE MONTH

Word Count:_____   Research Hours:_____
Brainstorming Hours:_____   Reading Hours:_____
Editing Hours:_____
Marketing Hours:_____

TOTAL FOR THE YEAR SO FAR

Word Count:_____   Research Hours:_____
Brainstorming Hours:_____   Reading Hours:_____
Editing Hours:_____
Marketing Hours:_____

Don't forget to color in your grid!

JUNE

You're moving into the halfway mark for the year. Take this time to truly evaluate what is working and not. If you need to change something and you have been putting it off, do it now! You still have time to meet or exceed your goals for this year. We believe in you!

Pride Month & Caribbean-America Heritage Month

Jun 6 D-Day
Jun 14 Flag Day

Jun 19 Father's Day & Juneteenth
Jun 21 June Solstice

WHAT DOES YOUR MONTH LOOK LIKE

Holidays:_____   Weekends:_____

Weekdays:_____   Other:_____

What **project(s)** do you plan on working on?

_____

What **goal** are you aiming to achieve?

_____

What will be your biggest **obstacle** this month?

_____

How will you **overcome** this? Or adjust for this?

_____

What will be your End of the Month **reward**?

_____

GOALS FOR THIS MONTH

Word Count:_____   Marketing Hours:_____

Brainstorming Hours:_____   Research Hours:_____

Editing Hours:_____   Reading Hours:_____

JUNE

JUNE

DAILY ACCOMPLISHMENTS   **WEDNESDAY 1**

*WORD COUNT:*_____   *MARKETING HOURS:*_____
*BRAINSTORMING HOURS:*_____   *RESEARCH HOURS:*_____
*EDITING HOURS:*_____   *READING HOURS:*_____

DAILY ACCOMPLISHMENTS   **THURSDAY 2**

*WORD COUNT:*_____   *MARKETING HOURS:*_____
*BRAINSTORMING HOURS:*_____   *RESEARCH HOURS:*_____
*EDITING HOURS:*_____   *READING HOURS:*_____

DAILY ACCOMPLISHMENTS   **FRIDAY 3**

*WORD COUNT:*_____   *MARKETING HOURS:*_____
*BRAINSTORMING HOURS:*_____   *RESEARCH HOURS:*_____
*EDITING HOURS:*_____   *READING HOURS:*_____

DAILY ACCOMPLISHMENTS   **SATURDAY 4**

*WORD COUNT:*_____   *MARKETING HOURS:*_____
*BRAINSTORMING HOURS:*_____   *RESEARCH HOURS:*_____
*EDITING HOURS:*_____   *READING HOURS:*_____

DAILY ACCOMPLISHMENTS   **SUNDAY 5**

*WORD COUNT:*_____   *MARKETING HOURS:*_____
*BRAINSTORMING HOURS:*_____   *RESEARCH HOURS:*_____
*EDITING HOURS:*_____   *READING HOURS:*_____

DAILY ACCOMPLISHMENTS   **MONDAY 6**

*WORD COUNT:*_____   *MARKETING HOURS:*_____
*BRAINSTORMING HOURS:*_____   *RESEARCH HOURS:*_____
*EDITING HOURS:*_____   *READING HOURS:*_____

DAILY ACCOMPLISHMENTS   **TUESDAY 7**

*WORD COUNT:*_____   *MARKETING HOURS:*_____
*BRAINSTORMING HOURS:*_____   *RESEARCH HOURS:*_____
*EDITING HOURS:*_____   *READING HOURS:*_____

Weekly Overview

EXERCISE: Take 5-minutes to write something with the 2 words below:

Mistake   Saucer

Post your exercise on the 4HP Accountable Authors Group on Facebook!

What was your sprint time and top word count?

_____

List a new song you discovered this week:

_____

Favorite food or drink this week:

_____

How did you reward yourself?

_____

What project(s) did you work on?

_____

What are you reading?

_____

What went well this week?

_____

What could improve this week?

_____

_____

_____

Total for the Week

Word Count:_____   Marketing Hours:_____
Brainstorming Hours:_____   Research Hours:_____
Editing Hours:_____   Reading Hours:_____

Don't forget to color in your grid!

The Cheerleader

Record a moment when you last succeeded. You did that? You can totally do this.

THE ARCHITECT

Post the blurb of your current project on the 4HP Accountable Authors group on Facebook.

THE RESEARCHER

Use maps, photos, and even Google Earth to get a sense of places you've never visited before writing about them. You don't want to miss a vital detail about the landscape.

THE TASKMASTER

Are you stuck? Go talk to someone, anyone, about your story. Even if they say nothing useful, talking it out will help you move forward. And who knows, you may find a Muse along the way.

JUNE

DAILY ACCOMPLISHMENTS   **WEDNESDAY 8**

*WORD COUNT:*_____   *MARKETING HOURS:*_____
*BRAINSTORMING HOURS:*_____   *RESEARCH HOURS:*_____
*EDITING HOURS:*_____   *READING HOURS:*_____

DAILY ACCOMPLISHMENTS   **THURSDAY 9**

*WORD COUNT:*_____   *MARKETING HOURS:*_____
*BRAINSTORMING HOURS:*_____   *RESEARCH HOURS:*_____
*EDITING HOURS:*_____   *READING HOURS:*_____

DAILY ACCOMPLISHMENTS   **FRIDAY 10**

*WORD COUNT:*_____   *MARKETING HOURS:*_____
*BRAINSTORMING HOURS:*_____   *RESEARCH HOURS:*_____
*EDITING HOURS:*_____   *READING HOURS:*_____

DAILY ACCOMPLISHMENTS   **SATURDAY 11**

*WORD COUNT:*_____   *MARKETING HOURS:*_____
*BRAINSTORMING HOURS:*_____   *RESEARCH HOURS:*_____
*EDITING HOURS:*_____   *READING HOURS:*_____

DAILY ACCOMPLISHMENTS   **SUNDAY 12**

*WORD COUNT:*_____   *MARKETING HOURS:*_____
*BRAINSTORMING HOURS:*_____   *RESEARCH HOURS:*_____
*EDITING HOURS:*_____   *READING HOURS:*_____

DAILY ACCOMPLISHMENTS   **MONDAY 13**

*WORD COUNT:*_____   *MARKETING HOURS:*_____
*BRAINSTORMING HOURS:*_____   *RESEARCH HOURS:*_____
*EDITING HOURS:*_____   *READING HOURS:*_____

DAILY ACCOMPLISHMENTS   **TUESDAY 14**

*WORD COUNT:*_____   *MARKETING HOURS:*_____
*BRAINSTORMING HOURS:*_____   *RESEARCH HOURS:*_____
*EDITING HOURS:*_____   *READING HOURS:*_____

JUNE

WEEKLY OVERVIEW

EXERCISE: Take 5-minutes to write something with the 2 words below:

Orchestra   Sofa

Post your exercise on the 4HP Accountable Authors Group on Facebook!

What was your sprint time and top word count?

_____

List a new song you discovered this week:

_____

Favorite food or drink this week:

_____

How did you reward yourself?

_____

What project(s) did you work on?

_____

What are you reading?

_____

What went well this week?

_____

What could improve this week?

_____

_____

_____

TOTAL FOR THE WEEK

Word Count:_____   Marketing Hours:_____
Brainstorming Hours:_____   Research Hours:_____
Editing Hours:_____   Reading Hours:_____

Don't forget to color in your grid!

The Cheerleader

Pick a color that describes the mood of your lead character right now! What is it?

THE ARCHITECT

Use comments as notes for your future self. Add thoughts if you are stuck--or to make sure you counted the right number of bullets to reload that gun.

THE RESEARCHER

"Know that the Creator lives and moves and breathes within you. So those dreams? Risk them. Those words? Write them. Those hopes? Believe them."
~ Elora Nicole Ramirez

THE TASKMASTER

Life will happen to you. Acknowledge it, understand it, then move on. Don't let it stop your creativity. Let it fuel you to create more.

JUNE

DAILY ACCOMPLISHMENTS   **WEDNESDAY 15**

WORD COUNT:_____   MARKETING HOURS:_____
BRAINSTORMING HOURS:_____   RESEARCH HOURS:_____
EDITING HOURS:_____   READING HOURS:_____

DAILY ACCOMPLISHMENTS   **THURSDAY 16**

WORD COUNT:_____   MARKETING HOURS:_____
BRAINSTORMING HOURS:_____   RESEARCH HOURS:_____
EDITING HOURS:_____   READING HOURS:_____

DAILY ACCOMPLISHMENTS   **FRIDAY 17**

WORD COUNT:_____   MARKETING HOURS:_____
BRAINSTORMING HOURS:_____   RESEARCH HOURS:_____
EDITING HOURS:_____   READING HOURS:_____

DAILY ACCOMPLISHMENTS   **SATURDAY 18**

WORD COUNT:_____   MARKETING HOURS:_____
BRAINSTORMING HOURS:_____   RESEARCH HOURS:_____
EDITING HOURS:_____   READING HOURS:_____

DAILY ACCOMPLISHMENTS   **SUNDAY 19**

WORD COUNT:_____   MARKETING HOURS:_____
BRAINSTORMING HOURS:_____   RESEARCH HOURS:_____
EDITING HOURS:_____   READING HOURS:_____

DAILY ACCOMPLISHMENTS   **MONDAY 20**

WORD COUNT:_____   MARKETING HOURS:_____
BRAINSTORMING HOURS:_____   RESEARCH HOURS:_____
EDITING HOURS:_____   READING HOURS:_____

DAILY ACCOMPLISHMENTS   **TUESDAY 21**

WORD COUNT:_____   MARKETING HOURS:_____
BRAINSTORMING HOURS:_____   RESEARCH HOURS:_____
EDITING HOURS:_____   READING HOURS:_____

JUNE

WEEKLY OVERVIEW

EXERCISE: Take 5-minutes to write something with the 2 words below:

Custard   Float

Post your exercise on the 4HP Accountable Authors Group on Facebook!

What was your sprint time and top word count?

_____

List a new song you discovered this week:

_____

Favorite food or drink this week:

_____

How did you reward yourself?

_____

What project(s) did you work on?

_____

What are you reading?

_____

What went well this week?

_____

What could improve this week?

_____

_____

_____

TOTAL FOR THE WEEK

Word Count:_____   Marketing Hours:_____
Brainstorming Hours:_____   Research Hours:_____
Editing Hours:_____   Reading Hours:_____

Don't forget to color in your grid!

The Cheerleader

When was the last time you visited a library? Do you have a library card? If you haven't been in a while, go check it out. Get into the habit of visiting once a month.

THE ARCHITECT

"All the words I use in my stories can be found in the dictionary—it's just a matter of arranging them into the right sentences."
~ Somerset Maugham

THE RESEARCHER

Trope Time: Research common tropes in your genre. How are you following or breaking these models?

THE TASKMASTER

Find out if your favorite author has advice on writing. Does it inspire you? It should. (If they don't have one, look up books by Stephen King, Jeff Strand & Gena Showalter.)

JUNE

Week 4

Daily Accomplishments — Wednesday 22

Word Count:_____

Brainstorming Hours:_____

Editing Hours:_____

Marketing Hours:_____

Research Hours:_____

Reading Hours:_____

Daily Accomplishments — Thursday 23

Word Count:_____

Brainstorming Hours:_____

Editing Hours:_____

Marketing Hours:_____

Research Hours:_____

Reading Hours:_____

Daily Accomplishments — Friday 24

Word Count:_____

Brainstorming Hours:_____

Editing Hours:_____

Marketing Hours:_____

Research Hours:_____

Reading Hours:_____

Daily Accomplishments — Saturday 25

Word Count:_____

Brainstorming Hours:_____

Editing Hours:_____

Marketing Hours:_____

Research Hours:_____

Reading Hours:_____

Daily Accomplishments — Sunday 26

Word Count:_____

Brainstorming Hours:_____

Editing Hours:_____

Marketing Hours:_____

Research Hours:_____

Reading Hours:_____

Daily Accomplishments — Monday 27

Word Count:_____

Brainstorming Hours:_____

Editing Hours:_____

Marketing Hours:_____

Research Hours:_____

Reading Hours:_____

Daily Accomplishments — Tuesday 28

Word Count:_____

Brainstorming Hours:_____

Editing Hours:_____

Marketing Hours:_____

Research Hours:_____

Reading Hours:_____

Weekly Overview

Exercise: Take 5-minutes to write something with the 2 words below:

Table   Laxative

Post your exercise on the 4HP Accountable Authors Group on Facebook!

What was your sprint time and top word count?

_____

List a new song you discovered this week:

_____

Favorite food or drink this week:

_____

How did you reward yourself?

_____

What project(s) did you work on?

_____

What are you reading?

_____

What went well this week?

_____

What could improve this week?

_____

_____

_____

Total for the Week

Word Count:_____   Marketing Hours:_____
Brainstorming Hours:_____   Research Hours:_____
Editing Hours:_____   Reading Hours:_____

Don't forget to color in your grid!

The Cheerleader

"Anyone who is going to be a writer knows enough at 15 to write several novels."

~ May Sarton

THE ARCHITECT

Best book to movie adaption. Justify it.

THE RESEARCHER

Feeling blocked? Use this time to do research, organize your notes, or focus on something else project-related, so your mind doesn't wander from the main task: writing.

THE TASKMASTER

Stop wondering if you're good enough. You are.

In fact, you are great.

So get over it and keep writing.

JUNE

125

DAILY ACCOMPLISHMENTS	WEDNESDAY 29
WORD COUNT:_____	MARKETING HOURS:_____
BRAINSTORMING HOURS:_____	RESEARCH HOURS:_____
EDITING HOURS:_____	READING HOURS:_____

DAILY ACCOMPLISHMENTS	THURSDAY 30
WORD COUNT:_____	MARKETING HOURS:_____
BRAINSTORMING HOURS:_____	RESEARCH HOURS:_____
EDITING HOURS:_____	READING HOURS:_____

JUNE

The Cheerleader

Stuff You Should Know: You're halfway there! If you were flying to the moon, you'd have traveled 180,000 km by now (*assuming the moon is at its closest point to the earth.*) June 30th is the 181st day of the year (*if it's not a leap year*), so that means you would've traveled 994.5 km each day to get where you are right now. That's nearly 619 miles so far--and the Proclaimers only made it 500! Keep going!

Weekly Overview

EXERCISE: Take 5-minutes to write something with the 2 words below:

Fashion   Lobster

Post your exercise on the 4HP Accountable Authors Group on Facebook!

What was your sprint time and top word count?

_____

List a new song you discovered this week:

_____

Favorite food or drink this week:

_____

How did you reward yourself?

_____

What project(s) did you work on?

_____

What are you reading?

_____

What went well this week?

_____

What could improve this week?

_____

_____

_____

Total for the Week

Word Count:_____   Marketing Hours:_____
Brainstorming Hours:_____   Research Hours:_____
Editing Hours:_____   Reading Hours:_____

Don't forget to color in your grid!

MONTHLY ACTIVITY GRID

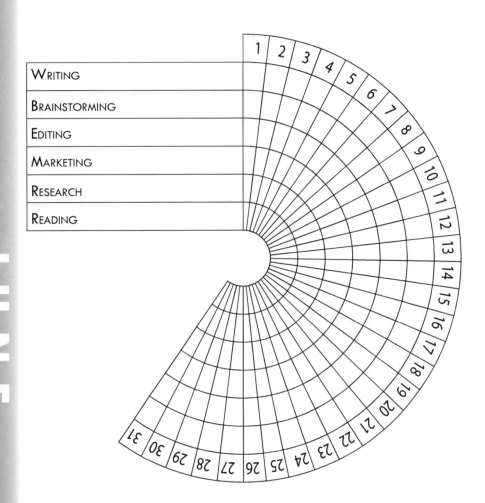

JUNE

| WRITING |
| BRAINSTORMING |
| EDITING |
| MARKETING |
| RESEARCH |
| READING |

YOUR AVERAGE WORD COUNT FOR THE MONTH

Total Word Count:_____ Divided by _____ days =_____

TOTAL FOR THE YEAR SO FAR

Word Count:_____ Marketing Hours:_____

Brainstorming Hours:_____ Research Hours:_____

Editing Hours:_____ Reading Hours:_____

JOURNAL

What was your **top week**?

_____

What made your **top week** successful?

_____

What was your biggest **obstacle**?

_____

How did you **overcome** this? Or could do better next time?

_____

_____

What was your biggest **achievement**?

_____

_____

What **inspired** you most this month?

_____

Did you **discover** a new writing tip or advice this month?

_____

_____

JUNE

TOTAL FOR THE MONTH

Word Count:_____   Research Hours:_____
Brainstorming Hours:_____   Reading Hours:_____
Editing Hours:_____
Marketing Hours:_____

TOTAL FOR THE YEAR SO FAR

Word Count:_____   Research Hours:_____
Brainstorming Hours:_____   Reading Hours:_____
Editing Hours:_____
Marketing Hours:_____

Don't forget to color in your grid!

JULY

This can be one of the most distracting times of year with fun in the sun. You can always go outside and write. Maybe even find a local coffee shop where the atmosphere is perfect to feel inspired and people watch at the same time.

Jul 4 Independence Day
Jul 14 Bastille Day

Jul 29 Dog Days of
Summer Starts

Jul 30 International Day of
Friendship

WHAT DOES YOUR MONTH LOOK LIKE

Holidays:_____   Weekends:_____
Weekdays:_____   Other:_____

What **project(s)** do you plan on working on?

_____

What **goal** are you aiming to achieve?

_____

What will be your biggest **obstacle** this month?

_____

How will you **overcome** this? Or adjust for this?

_____

What will be your End of the Month **reward**?

_____

GOALS FOR THIS MONTH

Word Count:_____   Marketing Hours:_____
Brainstorming Hours:_____   Research Hours:_____
Editing Hours:_____   Reading Hours:_____

131

WEEK 1

DAILY ACCOMPLISHMENTS   **FRIDAY 1**

WORD COUNT:_____   MARKETING HOURS:_____
BRAINSTORMING HOURS:_____   RESEARCH HOURS:_____
EDITING HOURS:_____   READING HOURS:_____

DAILY ACCOMPLISHMENTS   **SATURDAY 2**

WORD COUNT:_____   MARKETING HOURS:_____
BRAINSTORMING HOURS:_____   RESEARCH HOURS:_____
EDITING HOURS:_____   READING HOURS:_____

DAILY ACCOMPLISHMENTS   **SUNDAY 3**

WORD COUNT:_____   MARKETING HOURS:_____
BRAINSTORMING HOURS:_____   RESEARCH HOURS:_____
EDITING HOURS:_____   READING HOURS:_____

DAILY ACCOMPLISHMENTS   **MONDAY 4**

WORD COUNT:_____   MARKETING HOURS:_____
BRAINSTORMING HOURS:_____   RESEARCH HOURS:_____
EDITING HOURS:_____   READING HOURS:_____

DAILY ACCOMPLISHMENTS   **TUESDAY 5**

WORD COUNT:_____   MARKETING HOURS:_____
BRAINSTORMING HOURS:_____   RESEARCH HOURS:_____
EDITING HOURS:_____   READING HOURS:_____

DAILY ACCOMPLISHMENTS   **WEDNESDAY 6**

WORD COUNT:_____   MARKETING HOURS:_____
BRAINSTORMING HOURS:_____   RESEARCH HOURS:_____
EDITING HOURS:_____   READING HOURS:_____

DAILY ACCOMPLISHMENTS   **THURSDAY 7**

WORD COUNT:_____   MARKETING HOURS:_____
BRAINSTORMING HOURS:_____   RESEARCH HOURS:_____
EDITING HOURS:_____   READING HOURS:_____

WEEKLY OVERVIEW

EXERCISE: Take 5-minutes to write something with the 2 words below:

Saliva   Tortoise

Post your exercise on the 4HP Accountable Authors Group on Facebook!

What was your sprint time and top word count?

_____

List a new song you discovered this week:

_____

Favorite food or drink this week:

_____

How did you reward yourself?

_____

What project(s) did you work on?

_____

What are you reading?

_____

What went well this week?

_____

What could improve this week?

_____

_____

_____

TOTAL FOR THE WEEK

Word Count:_____   Marketing Hours:_____
Brainstorming Hours:_____   Research Hours:_____
Editing Hours:_____   Reading Hours:_____

Don't forget to color in your grid!

The Cheerleader

Name the last genre book
you read that's similar to
your current project.

THE ARCHITECT

Blurb Time: Revisit the blurb
for your current project.
Does this still work?

THE RESEARCHER

Are you writing about fossils? Blood spatter? Cuisine? Find an expert in that field and ask them to speak with you. You will be surprised how much they're willing to share.

THE TASKMASTER

Your work will not be perfect. Nothing is "perfect," so don't wait for that. Instead, keep improving by producing more work. That is the only way.

WEEK 2

DAILY ACCOMPLISHMENTS	**FRIDAY 8**
Word Count:	*Marketing Hours:*
Brainstorming Hours:	*Research Hours:*
Editing Hours:	*Reading Hours:*

DAILY ACCOMPLISHMENTS	**SATURDAY 9**
Word Count:	*Marketing Hours:*
Brainstorming Hours:	*Research Hours:*
Editing Hours:	*Reading Hours:*

DAILY ACCOMPLISHMENTS	**SUNDAY 10**
Word Count:	*Marketing Hours:*
Brainstorming Hours:	*Research Hours:*
Editing Hours:	*Reading Hours:*

DAILY ACCOMPLISHMENTS	**MONDAY 11**
Word Count:	*Marketing Hours:*
Brainstorming Hours:	*Research Hours:*
Editing Hours:	*Reading Hours:*

DAILY ACCOMPLISHMENTS	**TUESDAY 12**
Word Count:	*Marketing Hours:*
Brainstorming Hours:	*Research Hours:*
Editing Hours:	*Reading Hours:*

DAILY ACCOMPLISHMENTS	**WEDNESDAY 13**
Word Count:	*Marketing Hours:*
Brainstorming Hours:	*Research Hours:*
Editing Hours:	*Reading Hours:*

DAILY ACCOMPLISHMENTS	**THURSDAY 14**
Word Count:	*Marketing Hours:*
Brainstorming Hours:	*Research Hours:*
Editing Hours:	*Reading Hours:*

WEEKLY OVERVIEW

EXERCISE: Take 5-minutes to write something with the 2 words below:

Arthritis   Hooligan

Post your exercise on the 4HP Accountable Authors Group on Facebook!

What was your sprint time and top word count?

_____

List a new song you discovered this week:

_____

Favorite food or drink this week:

_____

How did you reward yourself?

_____

What project(s) did you work on?

_____

What are you reading?

_____

What went well this week?

_____

What could improve this week?

_____

_____

_____

TOTAL FOR THE WEEK

Word Count:_____   Marketing Hours:_____
Brainstorming Hours:_____   Research Hours:_____
Editing Hours:_____   Reading Hours:_____

Don't forget to color in your grid!

JULY

The Cheerleader

Social Media Time: Pay attention to the real world besides your project. Post meaningful content on social media that relates to your writing (share a book, link an article, post a meme, etc.)

THE ARCHITECT

Interview Time: Create a list of questions you'd like to ask a character in your project.

THE RESEARCHER

"If you write one story, it may be bad; if you write a hundred, you have the odds in your favor."

~ Edgar Rice Burroughs

THE TASKMASTER

"The world is a mess, and I just need to rule it."

~ Dr. Horrible (Dr. Horrible's Sing-a-Long Blog)

It is a mess, and your writing will inspire or provide an escape for your readers. So get a move on, use your hammer, and get it done.

DAILY ACCOMPLISHMENTS   **FRIDAY 15**

*WORD COUNT:*_____   *MARKETING HOURS:*_____
*BRAINSTORMING HOURS:*_____   *RESEARCH HOURS:*_____
*EDITING HOURS:*_____   *READING HOURS:*_____

DAILY ACCOMPLISHMENTS   **SATURDAY 16**

*WORD COUNT:*_____   *MARKETING HOURS:*_____
*BRAINSTORMING HOURS:*_____   *RESEARCH HOURS:*_____
*EDITING HOURS:*_____   *READING HOURS:*_____

DAILY ACCOMPLISHMENTS   **SUNDAY 17**

*WORD COUNT:*_____   *MARKETING HOURS:*_____
*BRAINSTORMING HOURS:*_____   *RESEARCH HOURS:*_____
*EDITING HOURS:*_____   *READING HOURS:*_____

DAILY ACCOMPLISHMENTS   **MONDAY 18**

*WORD COUNT:*_____   *MARKETING HOURS:*_____
*BRAINSTORMING HOURS:*_____   *RESEARCH HOURS:*_____
*EDITING HOURS:*_____   *READING HOURS:*_____

DAILY ACCOMPLISHMENTS   **TUESDAY 19**

*WORD COUNT:*_____   *MARKETING HOURS:*_____
*BRAINSTORMING HOURS:*_____   *RESEARCH HOURS:*_____
*EDITING HOURS:*_____   *READING HOURS:*_____

DAILY ACCOMPLISHMENTS   **WEDNESDAY 20**

*WORD COUNT:*_____   *MARKETING HOURS:*_____
*BRAINSTORMING HOURS:*_____   *RESEARCH HOURS:*_____
*EDITING HOURS:*_____   *READING HOURS:*_____

DAILY ACCOMPLISHMENTS   **THURSDAY 21**

*WORD COUNT:*_____   *MARKETING HOURS:*_____
*BRAINSTORMING HOURS:*_____   *RESEARCH HOURS:*_____
*EDITING HOURS:*_____   *READING HOURS:*_____

JULY

WEEKLY OVERVIEW

EXERCISE: Take 5-minutes to write something with the 2 words below:

Tattoo   Referee

Post your exercise on the 4HP Accountable Authors Group on Facebook!

What was your sprint time and top word count?

_____

List a new song you discovered this week:

_____

Favorite food or drink this week:

_____

How did you reward yourself?

_____

What project(s) did you work on?

_____

What are you reading?

_____

What went well this week?

_____

What could improve this week?

_____

_____

_____

TOTAL FOR THE WEEK

Word Count:_____   Marketing Hours:_____
Brainstorming Hours:_____   Research Hours:_____
Editing Hours:_____   Reading Hours:_____

Don't forget to color in your grid!

JULY

The Cheerleader

What's your favorite book of all time? Why?

THE ARCHITECT

"People on the outside think there's something magical about writing, that you go up in the attic at midnight and cast the bones and come down in the morning with a story, but it isn't like that. You sit in back of the typewriter and you work, and that's all there is to it."

~ Harlan Ellison

THE RESEARCHER

People-watching is a great way to inspire stories. But, hiding in the bushes using binoculars might be a bit much!

THE TASKMASTER

Okay. You are officially halfway through the year. How's it going? If you need to change something, do it. You can reset your goals so they are more reasonable, but you can also challenge yourself to surpass new ones.

JULY

DAILY ACCOMPLISHMENTS   **FRIDAY 22**

WORD COUNT:_____   MARKETING HOURS:_____
BRAINSTORMING HOURS:_____   RESEARCH HOURS:_____
EDITING HOURS:_____   READING HOURS:_____

DAILY ACCOMPLISHMENTS   **SATURDAY 23**

WORD COUNT:_____   MARKETING HOURS:_____
BRAINSTORMING HOURS:_____   RESEARCH HOURS:_____
EDITING HOURS:_____   READING HOURS:_____

DAILY ACCOMPLISHMENTS   **SUNDAY 24**

WORD COUNT:_____   MARKETING HOURS:_____
BRAINSTORMING HOURS:_____   RESEARCH HOURS:_____
EDITING HOURS:_____   READING HOURS:_____

DAILY ACCOMPLISHMENTS   **MONDAY 25**

WORD COUNT:_____   MARKETING HOURS:_____
BRAINSTORMING HOURS:_____   RESEARCH HOURS:_____
EDITING HOURS:_____   READING HOURS:_____

DAILY ACCOMPLISHMENTS   **TUESDAY 26**

WORD COUNT:_____   MARKETING HOURS:_____
BRAINSTORMING HOURS:_____   RESEARCH HOURS:_____
EDITING HOURS:_____   READING HOURS:_____

DAILY ACCOMPLISHMENTS   **WEDNESDAY 27**

WORD COUNT:_____   MARKETING HOURS:_____
BRAINSTORMING HOURS:_____   RESEARCH HOURS:_____
EDITING HOURS:_____   READING HOURS:_____

DAILY ACCOMPLISHMENTS   **THURSDAY 28**

WORD COUNT:_____   MARKETING HOURS:_____
BRAINSTORMING HOURS:_____   RESEARCH HOURS:_____
EDITING HOURS:_____   READING HOURS:_____

JULY

Weekly Overview

EXERCISE: Take 5-minutes to write something with the 2 words below:

Bargain   **Eyebrow**

Post your exercise on the 4HP Accountable Authors Group on Facebook!

What was your sprint time and top word count?

_____

List a new song you discovered this week:

_____

Favorite food or drink this week:

_____

How did you reward yourself?

_____

What project(s) did you work on?

_____

What are you reading?

_____

What went well this week?

_____

What could improve this week?

_____

_____

_____

Total for the Week

Word Count:_____   Marketing Hours:_____
Brainstorming Hours:_____   Research Hours:_____
Editing Hours:_____   Reading Hours:_____

Don't forget to color in your grid!

JULY

The Cheerleader

"People say, 'What advice do you have for people who want to be writers?' I say, they don't really need advice, they know they want to be writers, and they're gonna do it. Those people who know that they really want to do this and are cut out for it, they know it."

~ R.L. Stine

THE ARCHITECT

Use dolls to act out fight scenes (or even sex scenes) to ensure body parts are in the right places.

THE RESEARCHER

Research real religions, climates, maps, and political structures to help inspire your worldbuilding. This is especially important if you're writing fantasy but can still be incorporated in contemporary works.

THE TASKMASTER

Are you jealous of other writers' accomplishments? Trust me--there're those who are jealous of you. Remember, you're someone else's inspiration; you just might not see it yet.

DAILY ACCOMPLISHMENTS   **FRIDAY 29**

*WORD COUNT:*_____   *MARKETING HOURS:*_____
*BRAINSTORMING HOURS:*_____   *RESEARCH HOURS:*_____
*EDITING HOURS:*_____   *READING HOURS:*_____

DAILY ACCOMPLISHMENTS   **SATURDAY 30**

*WORD COUNT:*_____   *MARKETING HOURS:*_____
*BRAINSTORMING HOURS:*_____   *RESEARCH HOURS:*_____
*EDITING HOURS:*_____   *READING HOURS:*_____

DAILY ACCOMPLISHMENTS   **SUNDAY 31**

*WORD COUNT:*_____   *MARKETING HOURS:*_____
*BRAINSTORMING HOURS:*_____   *RESEARCH HOURS:*_____
*EDITING HOURS:*_____   *READING HOURS:*_____

THE ARCHITECT

It's time to declare your independence from bad habits and wasted time. It is easy to get distracted. Make sure you and your project are a priority. Have you been doing your sprints? If not, this is a good time to add them to your schedule.

WEEKLY OVERVIEW

EXERCISE: Take 5-minutes to write something with the 2 words below:

Marble   Fly

Post your exercise on the 4HP Accountable Authors Group on Facebook!

What was your sprint time and top word count?

_____

List a new song you discovered this week:

_____

Favorite food or drink this week:

_____

How did you reward yourself?

_____

What project(s) did you work on?

_____

What are you reading?

_____

What went well this week?

_____

What could improve this week?

_____

_____

_____

TOTAL FOR THE WEEK

Word Count:_____   Marketing Hours:_____
Brainstorming Hours:_____   Research Hours:_____
Editing Hours:_____   Reading Hours:_____

Don't forget to color in your grid!

MONTHLY ACTIVITY GRID

JULY

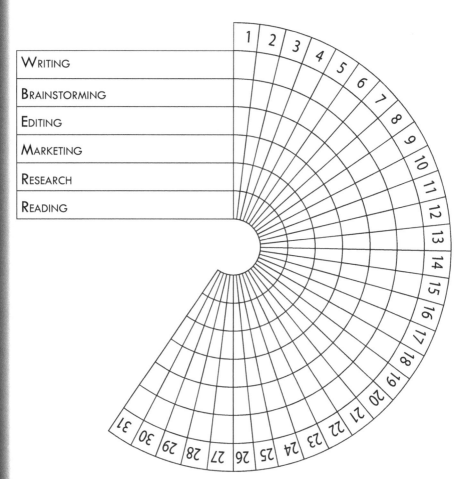

WRITING

BRAINSTORMING

EDITING

MARKETING

RESEARCH

READING

YOUR AVERAGE WORD COUNT FOR THE MONTH

Total Word Count:_____ Divided by _____ days =_____

TOTAL FOR THE YEAR SO FAR

Word Count:_____   Marketing Hours:_____

Brainstorming Hours:_____   Research Hours:_____

Editing Hours:_____   Reading Hours:_____

JOURNAL

What was your **top week**?

_____

What made your **top week** successful?

_____

What was your biggest **obstacle**?

_____

How did you **overcome** this? Or could do better next time?

_____

_____

What was your biggest **achievement**?

_____

_____

What **inspired** you most this month?

_____

Did you **discover** a new writing tip or advice this month?

_____

_____

TOTAL FOR THE MONTH

Word Count:_____ Research Hours:_____
Brainstorming Hours:_____ Reading Hours:_____
Editing Hours:_____
Marketing Hours:_____

TOTAL FOR THE YEAR SO FAR

Word Count:_____ Research Hours:_____
Brainstorming Hours:_____ Reading Hours:_____
Editing Hours:_____
Marketing Hours:_____

Don't forget to color in your grid!

AUGUST

School is coming soon. Have you thought about some creative writing classes? You do not have to be "in college" to take them. Also, you can find different writing workshops both online and in person. Knowledge is power. Make sure you are constantly learning even more skills as an author.

Aug 7 Purple Heart Day

Aug 19 World Humanitarian Day
Aug 21 National Senior Citizens Day

Aug 26 Women's Equality Day

WHAT DOES YOUR MONTH LOOK LIKE

Holidays:_____   Weekends:_____
Weekdays:_____   Other:_____

What **project(s)** do you plan on working on?

_____

What **goal** are you aiming to achieve?

_____

What will be your biggest **obstacle** this month?

_____

How will you **overcome** this? Or adjust for this?

_____

What will be your End of the Month **reward**?

_____

GOALS FOR THIS MONTH

Word Count:_____   Marketing Hours:_____
Brainstorming Hours:_____   Research Hours:_____
Editing Hours:_____   Reading Hours:_____

WEEK 1

DAILY ACCOMPLISHMENTS   MONDAY 1

WORD COUNT:_____   MARKETING HOURS:_____
BRAINSTORMING HOURS:_____   RESEARCH HOURS:_____
EDITING HOURS:_____   READING HOURS:_____

DAILY ACCOMPLISHMENTS   TUESDAY 2

WORD COUNT:_____   MARKETING HOURS:_____
BRAINSTORMING HOURS:_____   RESEARCH HOURS:_____
EDITING HOURS:_____   READING HOURS:_____

DAILY ACCOMPLISHMENTS   WEDNESDAY 3

WORD COUNT:_____   MARKETING HOURS:_____
BRAINSTORMING HOURS:_____   RESEARCH HOURS:_____
EDITING HOURS:_____   READING HOURS:_____

DAILY ACCOMPLISHMENTS   THURSDAY 4

WORD COUNT:_____   MARKETING HOURS:_____
BRAINSTORMING HOURS:_____   RESEARCH HOURS:_____
EDITING HOURS:_____   READING HOURS:_____

DAILY ACCOMPLISHMENTS   FRIDAY 5

WORD COUNT:_____   MARKETING HOURS:_____
BRAINSTORMING HOURS:_____   RESEARCH HOURS:_____
EDITING HOURS:_____   READING HOURS:_____

DAILY ACCOMPLISHMENTS   SATURDAY 6

WORD COUNT:_____   MARKETING HOURS:_____
BRAINSTORMING HOURS:_____   RESEARCH HOURS:_____
EDITING HOURS:_____   READING HOURS:_____

DAILY ACCOMPLISHMENTS   SUNDAY 7

WORD COUNT:_____   MARKETING HOURS:_____
BRAINSTORMING HOURS:_____   RESEARCH HOURS:_____
EDITING HOURS:_____   READING HOURS:_____

Weekly Overview

EXERCISE: Take 5-minutes to write something with the 2 words below:

Fuse   Vase

Post your exercise on the 4HP Accountable Authors Group on Facebook!

What was your sprint time and top word count?

_____

List a new song you discovered this week:

_____

Favorite food or drink this week:

_____

How did you reward yourself?

_____

What project(s) did you work on?

_____

What are you reading?

_____

What went well this week?

_____

What could improve this week?

_____

_____

_____

TOTAL FOR THE WEEK

Word Count:_____   Marketing Hours:_____

Brainstorming Hours:_____   Research Hours:_____

Editing Hours:_____   Reading Hours:_____

Don't forget to color in your grid!

The Cheerleader

Make a list of "Never have I ever" items that you wish to accomplish as a writer.

THE ARCHITECT

"Any man who keeps working is not a failure. He may not be a great writer, but if he applies the old-fashioned virtues of hard, constant labor, he'll eventually make some kind of career for himself as writer."

~ Ray Bradbury

AUGUST

THE RESEARCHER

If you're writing about something outside of your experience, make sure to have several beta readers of that particular group read and critique. Example: Male writing from a female POV. Straight person writing from an LGBTQ+ POV, etc.

THE TASKMASTER

About three things I am absolutely certain:

1) You are awesome!
2) You can reach your goals!
3) Most important, the fans hunger for your words!

Never lose sight of that. (And Edward is a vampire.)

WEEK 2

DAILY ACCOMPLISHMENTS   **MONDAY 8**

*WORD COUNT:*_____   *MARKETING HOURS:*_____
*BRAINSTORMING HOURS:*_____   *RESEARCH HOURS:*_____
*EDITING HOURS:*_____   *READING HOURS:*_____

DAILY ACCOMPLISHMENTS   **TUESDAY 9**

*WORD COUNT:*_____   *MARKETING HOURS:*_____
*BRAINSTORMING HOURS:*_____   *RESEARCH HOURS:*_____
*EDITING HOURS:*_____   *READING HOURS:*_____

DAILY ACCOMPLISHMENTS   **WEDNESDAY 10**

*WORD COUNT:*_____   *MARKETING HOURS:*_____
*BRAINSTORMING HOURS:*_____   *RESEARCH HOURS:*_____
*EDITING HOURS:*_____   *READING HOURS:*_____

DAILY ACCOMPLISHMENTS   **THURSDAY 11**

*WORD COUNT:*_____   *MARKETING HOURS:*_____
*BRAINSTORMING HOURS:*_____   *RESEARCH HOURS:*_____
*EDITING HOURS:*_____   *READING HOURS:*_____

DAILY ACCOMPLISHMENTS   **FRIDAY 12**

*WORD COUNT:*_____   *MARKETING HOURS:*_____
*BRAINSTORMING HOURS:*_____   *RESEARCH HOURS:*_____
*EDITING HOURS:*_____   *READING HOURS:*_____

DAILY ACCOMPLISHMENTS   **SATURDAY 13**

*WORD COUNT:*_____   *MARKETING HOURS:*_____
*BRAINSTORMING HOURS:*_____   *RESEARCH HOURS:*_____
*EDITING HOURS:*_____   *READING HOURS:*_____

DAILY ACCOMPLISHMENTS   **SUNDAY 14**

*WORD COUNT:*_____   *MARKETING HOURS:*_____
*BRAINSTORMING HOURS:*_____   *RESEARCH HOURS:*_____
*EDITING HOURS:*_____   *READING HOURS:*_____

Weekly Overview

Exercise: Take 5-minutes to write something with the 2 words below:

Blue   Glue

Post your exercise on the 4HP Accountable Authors Group on Facebook!

What was your sprint time and top word count?

_____

List a new song you discovered this week:

_____

Favorite food or drink this week:

_____

How did you reward yourself?

_____

What project(s) did you work on?

_____

What are you reading?

_____

What went well this week?

_____

What could improve this week?

_____

_____

_____

AUGUST

Total for the Week

Word Count:_____   Marketing Hours:_____
Brainstorming Hours:_____   Research Hours:_____
Editing Hours:_____   Reading Hours:_____

Don't forget to color in your grid!

The Cheerleader

Find someone who overcame a challenge. Screenshot their picture. Make it the background image on your phone for a day.

THE ARCHITECT

Summary Check-in: Review your current project's summary. Does it still reflect the current iteration of your project?

THE RESEARCHER

"The most beautiful things are those that madness prompts and reason writes."

~ Andre Gide

THE TASKMASTER

Find your top word count for a day. Then take a day this week and write more than that. Your abilities will amaze you if you stop doubting them.

AUGUST

WEEK 3

DAILY ACCOMPLISHMENTS	**MONDAY 15**

Word Count: _____
Brainstorming Hours: _____
Editing Hours: _____

Marketing Hours: _____
Research Hours: _____
Reading Hours: _____

DAILY ACCOMPLISHMENTS	**TUESDAY 16**

Word Count: _____
Brainstorming Hours: _____
Editing Hours: _____

Marketing Hours: _____
Research Hours: _____
Reading Hours: _____

DAILY ACCOMPLISHMENTS	**WEDNESDAY 17**

Word Count: _____
Brainstorming Hours: _____
Editing Hours: _____

Marketing Hours: _____
Research Hours: _____
Reading Hours: _____

DAILY ACCOMPLISHMENTS	**THURSDAY 18**

Word Count: _____
Brainstorming Hours: _____
Editing Hours: _____

Marketing Hours: _____
Research Hours: _____
Reading Hours: _____

DAILY ACCOMPLISHMENTS	**FRIDAY 19**

Word Count: _____
Brainstorming Hours: _____
Editing Hours: _____

Marketing Hours: _____
Research Hours: _____
Reading Hours: _____

DAILY ACCOMPLISHMENTS	**SATURDAY 20**

Word Count: _____
Brainstorming Hours: _____
Editing Hours: _____

Marketing Hours: _____
Research Hours: _____
Reading Hours: _____

DAILY ACCOMPLISHMENTS	**SUNDAY 21**

Word Count: _____
Brainstorming Hours: _____
Editing Hours: _____

Marketing Hours: _____
Research Hours: _____
Reading Hours: _____

WEEKLY OVERVIEW

EXERCISE: Take 5-minutes to write something with the 2 words below:

Duct Tape   Epidemic

Post your exercise on the 4HP Accountable Authors Group on Facebook!

What was your sprint time and top word count?

_____

List a new song you discovered this week:

_____

Favorite food or drink this week:

_____

How did you reward yourself?

_____

What project(s) did you work on?

_____

What are you reading?

_____

What went well this week?

_____

What could improve this week?

_____

_____

_____

TOTAL FOR THE WEEK

Word Count:_____   Marketing Hours:_____
Brainstorming Hours:_____   Research Hours:_____
Editing Hours:_____   Reading Hours:_____

Don't forget to color in your grid!

AUGUST

The Cheerleader

"All we have to decide is what to do with the time that is given to us."
~ Gandalf (Lord of the Rings)

THE ARCHITECT

Switch gears and work on a different project this week. How did it go?

THE RESEARCHER

The Roman Naval fleet lost most of its ships during the same earthquake that knocked Helike into the sea!
Set a timer for 10 minutes and write a scene or poem with a tidal wave!

THE TASKMASTER

Every day, do something that scares you. Comfort zones make you complacent. Life is an adventure; don't wait for it to come to you.

AUGUST

DAILY ACCOMPLISHMENTS   MONDAY 22

WORD COUNT:_____   MARKETING HOURS:_____
BRAINSTORMING HOURS:_____   RESEARCH HOURS:_____
EDITING HOURS:_____   READING HOURS:_____

DAILY ACCOMPLISHMENTS   TUESDAY 23

WORD COUNT:_____   MARKETING HOURS:_____
BRAINSTORMING HOURS:_____   RESEARCH HOURS:_____
EDITING HOURS:_____   READING HOURS:_____

DAILY ACCOMPLISHMENTS   WEDNESDAY 24

WORD COUNT:_____   MARKETING HOURS:_____
BRAINSTORMING HOURS:_____   RESEARCH HOURS:_____
EDITING HOURS:_____   READING HOURS:_____

DAILY ACCOMPLISHMENTS   THURSDAY 25

WORD COUNT:_____   MARKETING HOURS:_____
BRAINSTORMING HOURS:_____   RESEARCH HOURS:_____
EDITING HOURS:_____   READING HOURS:_____

DAILY ACCOMPLISHMENTS   FRIDAY 26

WORD COUNT:_____   MARKETING HOURS:_____
BRAINSTORMING HOURS:_____   RESEARCH HOURS:_____
EDITING HOURS:_____   READING HOURS:_____

DAILY ACCOMPLISHMENTS   SATURDAY 27

WORD COUNT:_____   MARKETING HOURS:_____
BRAINSTORMING HOURS:_____   RESEARCH HOURS:_____
EDITING HOURS:_____   READING HOURS:_____

DAILY ACCOMPLISHMENTS   SUNDAY 28

WORD COUNT:_____   MARKETING HOURS:_____
BRAINSTORMING HOURS:_____   RESEARCH HOURS:_____
EDITING HOURS:_____   READING HOURS:_____

AUGUST

WEEKLY OVERVIEW

EXERCISE: Take 5-minutes to write something with the 2 words below:

Fad   Panic

Post your exercise on the 4HP Accountable Authors Group on Facebook!

What was your sprint time and top word count?

_____

List a new song you discovered this week:

_____

Favorite food or drink this week:

_____

How did you reward yourself?

_____

What project(s) did you work on?

_____

What are you reading?

_____

What went well this week?

_____

What could improve this week?

_____

_____

_____

TOTAL FOR THE WEEK

Word Count:_____   Marketing Hours:_____
Brainstorming Hours:_____   Research Hours:_____
Editing Hours:_____   Reading Hours:_____

Don't forget to color in your grid!

AUGUST

The Cheerleader

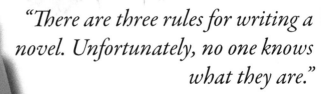

"There are three rules for writing a novel. Unfortunately, no one knows what they are."

~ W. Somerset Maugham

THE ARCHITECT

Read widely and often. It's a great way to build your internal editor.

THE RESEARCHER

Big Picture Time: Step back and craft a visual of your project. This could be a timeline of events, a layout of connections between characters, a world overview, or anything related to the entire package.

THE TASKMASTER

When was the last time you read your writing out loud? Find an open mic, go and read. You may be nervous, but hearing your words out loud is a very good idea.

AUGUST

DAILY ACCOMPLISHMENTS   MONDAY 29

WORD COUNT:_____   MARKETING HOURS:_____
BRAINSTORMING HOURS:_____   RESEARCH HOURS:_____
EDITING HOURS:_____   READING HOURS:_____

DAILY ACCOMPLISHMENTS   TUESDAY 30

WORD COUNT:_____   MARKETING HOURS:_____
BRAINSTORMING HOURS:_____   RESEARCH HOURS:_____
EDITING HOURS:_____   READING HOURS:_____

DAILY ACCOMPLISHMENTS   WEDNESDAY 31

WORD COUNT:_____   MARKETING HOURS:_____
BRAINSTORMING HOURS:_____   RESEARCH HOURS:_____
EDITING HOURS:_____   READING HOURS:_____

THE RESEARCHER

The beginning of fall is fast approaching. Make sure
not to fall back on your writing. See what
I did there? A pun just for you! How is
your knowledge acquistion going?
Are you spending time learning some
tricks of the trade that you can apply?
Good if you are, and you'd better
get that going if you are not! This is
all about you.

Weekly Overview

EXERCISE: Take 5-minutes to write something with the 2 words below:

Retro   Hammer

Post your exercise on the 4HP Accountable Authors Group on Facebook!

What was your sprint time and top word count?

_____

List a new song you discovered this week:

_____

Favorite food or drink this week:

_____

How did you reward yourself?

_____

What project(s) did you work on?

_____

What are you reading?

_____

What went well this week?

_____

What could improve this week?

_____

_____

_____

TOTAL FOR THE WEEK

Word Count:_____   Marketing Hours:_____
Brainstorming Hours:_____   Research Hours:_____
Editing Hours:_____   Reading Hours:_____

Don't forget to color in your grid!

MONTHLY ACTIVITY GRID

AUGUST

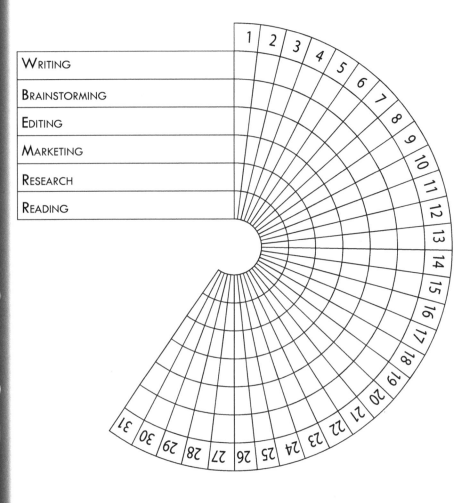

WRITING

BRAINSTORMING

EDITING

MARKETING

RESEARCH

READING

YOUR AVERAGE WORD COUNT FOR THE MONTH

Total Word Count:_____ Divided by _____ days =_____

TOTAL FOR THE YEAR SO FAR

Word Count:_____   Marketing Hours:_____

Brainstorming Hours:_____   Research Hours:_____

Editing Hours:_____   Reading Hours:_____

JOURNAL

What was your **top week**?

_____

What made your **top week** successful?

_____

What was your biggest **obstacle**?

_____

How did you **overcome** this? Or could do better next time?

_____

_____

What was your biggest **achievement**?

_____

_____

What **inspired** you most this month?

_____

Did you **discover** a new writing tip or advice this month?

_____

_____

_____

A U G U S T

TOTAL FOR THE MONTH

Word Count:_____   Research Hours:_____
Brainstorming Hours:_____   Reading Hours:_____
Editing Hours:_____
Marketing Hours:_____

TOTAL FOR THE YEAR SO FAR

Word Count:_____   Research Hours:_____
Brainstorming Hours:_____   Reading Hours:_____
Editing Hours:_____
Marketing Hours:_____

Don't forget to color in your grid!

SEPTEMBER

School has started again. You might be one of the many hitting the books or helping others to do so. Make sure you do not lose the good habits you formed. Also, this is a great time to find a local writers group. Finding like-minded people in your area or online is one of the most helpful things you can do. Also, don't forget to buy your 2022 Authors Accountability Guide!

Sep 5 Labor Day & The Researcher's Bday
Sep 11 First Responders Day

Sep 13 International Programmer's Day
Sep 21 International Day of Peace

Sep 22 Equinox
Sep 28 World Rabies Day

WHAT DOES YOUR MONTH LOOK LIKE

Holidays:_____   Weekends:_____
Weekdays:_____   Other:_____

What **project(s)** do you plan on working on?

_____

What **goal** are you aiming to achieve?

_____

What will be your biggest **obstacle** this month?

_____

How will you **overcome** this? Or adjust for this?

_____

What will be your End of the Month **reward**?

_____

GOALS FOR THIS MONTH

Word Count:_____   Marketing Hours:_____
Brainstorming Hours:_____   Research Hours:_____
Editing Hours:_____   Reading Hours:_____

WEEK 1

DAILY ACCOMPLISHMENTS   **THURSDAY 1**

WORD COUNT: _____   *MARKETING HOURS:* _____
BRAINSTORMING HOURS: _____   *RESEARCH HOURS:* _____
EDITING HOURS: _____   *READING HOURS:* _____

DAILY ACCOMPLISHMENTS   **FRIDAY 2**

WORD COUNT: _____   *MARKETING HOURS:* _____
BRAINSTORMING HOURS: _____   *RESEARCH HOURS:* _____
EDITING HOURS: _____   *READING HOURS:* _____

DAILY ACCOMPLISHMENTS   **SATURDAY 3**

WORD COUNT: _____   *MARKETING HOURS:* _____
BRAINSTORMING HOURS: _____   *RESEARCH HOURS:* _____
EDITING HOURS: _____   *READING HOURS:* _____

DAILY ACCOMPLISHMENTS   **SUNDAY 4**

WORD COUNT: _____   *MARKETING HOURS:* _____
BRAINSTORMING HOURS: _____   *RESEARCH HOURS:* _____
EDITING HOURS: _____   *READING HOURS:* _____

DAILY ACCOMPLISHMENTS   **MONDAY 5**

WORD COUNT: _____   *MARKETING HOURS:* _____
BRAINSTORMING HOURS: _____   *RESEARCH HOURS:* _____
EDITING HOURS: _____   *READING HOURS:* _____

DAILY ACCOMPLISHMENTS   **TUESDAY 6**

WORD COUNT: _____   *MARKETING HOURS:* _____
BRAINSTORMING HOURS: _____   *RESEARCH HOURS:* _____
EDITING HOURS: _____   *READING HOURS:* _____

DAILY ACCOMPLISHMENTS   **WEDNESDAY 7**

WORD COUNT: _____   *MARKETING HOURS:* _____
BRAINSTORMING HOURS: _____   *RESEARCH HOURS:* _____
EDITING HOURS: _____   *READING HOURS:* _____

WEEKLY OVERVIEW

What was your sprint time and top word count?

_____

List a new song you discovered this week:

_____

Favorite food or drink this week:

_____

How did you reward yourself?

_____

What project(s) did you work on?

_____

What are you reading?

_____

What went well this week?

_____

What could improve this week?

_____

_____

_____

TOTAL FOR THE WEEK

Word Count:_____   Marketing Hours:_____
Brainstorming Hours:_____   Research Hours:_____
Editing Hours:_____   Reading Hours:_____

Don't forget to color in your grid!

SEPTEMBER

The Cheerleader

Do you keep notes about your characters? Make sure to track details about them and their relationships.

THE ARCHITECT

Plot Holes Everywhere: What plot issues are you struggling with right now? Jot down possible stopgaps to explain the events.

THE RESEARCHER

Write a story about a character or creature that that has a strange anatomy quirk. A shrimp's heart is in their head, cows have four stomachs, and slugs have four noses. Your turn!

THE TASKMASTER

What's your worst fear as a writer? Write it down on paper. Then rip it to shreds or burn it. Good-- you're done with that now. Move forward.

Week 2

DAILY ACCOMPLISHMENTS   THURSDAY 8

WORD COUNT:_____   MARKETING HOURS:_____
BRAINSTORMING HOURS:_____   RESEARCH HOURS:_____
EDITING HOURS:_____   READING HOURS:_____

DAILY ACCOMPLISHMENTS   FRIDAY 9

WORD COUNT:_____   MARKETING HOURS:_____
BRAINSTORMING HOURS:_____   RESEARCH HOURS:_____
EDITING HOURS:_____   READING HOURS:_____

DAILY ACCOMPLISHMENTS   SATURDAY 10

WORD COUNT:_____   MARKETING HOURS:_____
BRAINSTORMING HOURS:_____   RESEARCH HOURS:_____
EDITING HOURS:_____   READING HOURS:_____

DAILY ACCOMPLISHMENTS   SUNDAY 11

WORD COUNT:_____   MARKETING HOURS:_____
BRAINSTORMING HOURS:_____   RESEARCH HOURS:_____
EDITING HOURS:_____   READING HOURS:_____

DAILY ACCOMPLISHMENTS   MONDAY 12

WORD COUNT:_____   MARKETING HOURS:_____
BRAINSTORMING HOURS:_____   RESEARCH HOURS:_____
EDITING HOURS:_____   READING HOURS:_____

DAILY ACCOMPLISHMENTS   TUESDAY 13

WORD COUNT:_____   MARKETING HOURS:_____
BRAINSTORMING HOURS:_____   RESEARCH HOURS:_____
EDITING HOURS:_____   READING HOURS:_____

DAILY ACCOMPLISHMENTS   WEDNESDAY 14

WORD COUNT:_____   MARKETING HOURS:_____
BRAINSTORMING HOURS:_____   RESEARCH HOURS:_____
EDITING HOURS:_____   READING HOURS:_____

WEEKLY OVERVIEW

EXERCISE: Take 5-minutes to write something with the 2 words below:

Tar   Gopher

Post your exercise on the 4HP Accountable Authors Group on Facebook!

What was your sprint time and top word count?

_____

List a new song you discovered this week:

_____

Favorite food or drink this week:

_____

How did you reward yourself?

_____

What project(s) did you work on?

_____

What are you reading?

_____

What went well this week?

_____

What could improve this week?

_____

_____

_____

TOTAL FOR THE WEEK

Word Count:_____   Marketing Hours:_____
Brainstorming Hours:_____   Research Hours:_____
Editing Hours:_____   Reading Hours:_____

Don't forget to color in your grid!

The Cheerleader

Write a piece of flash fiction (1000 words or less) and post it on your social media. Put the title here.

THE ARCHITECT

Vocab Building Time: Learn five new words. Flip through a dictionary, scroll through an online dictionary-- whatever works for you.

SEPTEMBER

THE RESEARCHER

"Don't expect the puppets of your mind to become the people of your story. If they are not realities in your own mind, there is no mysterious alchemy in ink and paper that will turn wooden figures into flesh and blood."

~ Leslie Gordon Barnard

THE TASKMASTER

Remember, you will find that people like to share stories. If you're writing about someone from a different background or place, then find someone from there and ask questions. Make your charaters feel more real.

DAILY ACCOMPLISHMENTS   **THURSDAY 15**

*WORD COUNT:*_____   *MARKETING HOURS:*_____
*BRAINSTORMING HOURS:*_____   *RESEARCH HOURS:*_____
*EDITING HOURS:*_____   *READING HOURS:*_____

DAILY ACCOMPLISHMENTS   **FRIDAY 16**

*WORD COUNT:*_____   *MARKETING HOURS:*_____
*BRAINSTORMING HOURS:*_____   *RESEARCH HOURS:*_____
*EDITING HOURS:*_____   *READING HOURS:*_____

DAILY ACCOMPLISHMENTS   **SATURDAY 17**

*WORD COUNT:*_____   *MARKETING HOURS:*_____
*BRAINSTORMING HOURS:*_____   *RESEARCH HOURS:*_____
*EDITING HOURS:*_____   *READING HOURS:*_____

DAILY ACCOMPLISHMENTS   **SUNDAY 18**

*WORD COUNT:*_____   *MARKETING HOURS:*_____
*BRAINSTORMING HOURS:*_____   *RESEARCH HOURS:*_____
*EDITING HOURS:*_____   *READING HOURS:*_____

DAILY ACCOMPLISHMENTS   **MONDAY 19**

*WORD COUNT:*_____   *MARKETING HOURS:*_____
*BRAINSTORMING HOURS:*_____   *RESEARCH HOURS:*_____
*EDITING HOURS:*_____   *READING HOURS:*_____

DAILY ACCOMPLISHMENTS   **TUESDAY 20**

*WORD COUNT:*_____   *MARKETING HOURS:*_____
*BRAINSTORMING HOURS:*_____   *RESEARCH HOURS:*_____
*EDITING HOURS:*_____   *READING HOURS:*_____

DAILY ACCOMPLISHMENTS   **WEDNESDAY 21**

*WORD COUNT:*_____   *MARKETING HOURS:*_____
*BRAINSTORMING HOURS:*_____   *RESEARCH HOURS:*_____
*EDITING HOURS:*_____   *READING HOURS:*_____

SEPTEMBER

Weekly Overview

EXERCISE: Take 5-minutes to write something with the 2 words below:

Startle   Mint

Post your exercise on the 4HP Accountable Authors Group on Facebook!

What was your sprint time and top word count?

_____

List a new song you discovered this week:

_____

Favorite food or drink this week:

_____

How did you reward yourself?

_____

What project(s) did you work on?

_____

What are you reading?

_____

What went well this week?

_____

What could improve this week?

_____

_____

_____

Total for the Week

Word Count:_____   Marketing Hours:_____
Brainstorming Hours:_____   Research Hours:_____
Editing Hours:_____   Reading Hours:_____

Don't forget to color in your grid!

SEPTEMBER

The Cheerleader

Don't wait. The timing will never be just right.

THE ARCHITECT

"It is perfectly okay to write garbage—as long as you edit brilliantly."

~ C. J. Cherryh

THE RESEARCHER

Self care reminder - Take a nap or plan to sleep properly this week. On that note, a student managed to stay away for 264.4 hours (11 days). His name? Randy Gardner s high school student in San Diego, CA in 1964! He set the record for longerst sleeplessness and fully recovered from this amazing feat!

THE TASKMASTER

Did you know Bill Gates recommends using five hours a week to continue learning? You can always gain more knowledge about your craft. Start a book on writing by a successful writer, take a webinar, or listen to a podcast (Like Drinking with Authors).

WEEK 4

DAILY ACCOMPLISHMENTS   **THURSDAY 22**

WORD COUNT:_____   MARKETING HOURS:_____

BRAINSTORMING HOURS:_____   RESEARCH HOURS:_____

EDITING HOURS:_____   READING HOURS:_____

DAILY ACCOMPLISHMENTS   **FRIDAY 23**

WORD COUNT:_____   MARKETING HOURS:_____

BRAINSTORMING HOURS:_____   RESEARCH HOURS:_____

EDITING HOURS:_____   READING HOURS:_____

DAILY ACCOMPLISHMENTS   **SATURDAY 24**

WORD COUNT:_____   MARKETING HOURS:_____

BRAINSTORMING HOURS:_____   RESEARCH HOURS:_____

EDITING HOURS:_____   READING HOURS:_____

DAILY ACCOMPLISHMENTS   **SUNDAY 25**

WORD COUNT:_____   MARKETING HOURS:_____

BRAINSTORMING HOURS:_____   RESEARCH HOURS:_____

EDITING HOURS:_____   READING HOURS:_____

DAILY ACCOMPLISHMENTS   **MONDAY 26**

WORD COUNT:_____   MARKETING HOURS:_____

BRAINSTORMING HOURS:_____   RESEARCH HOURS:_____

EDITING HOURS:_____   READING HOURS:_____

DAILY ACCOMPLISHMENTS   **TUESDAY 27**

WORD COUNT:_____   MARKETING HOURS:_____

BRAINSTORMING HOURS:_____   RESEARCH HOURS:_____

EDITING HOURS:_____   READING HOURS:_____

DAILY ACCOMPLISHMENTS   **WEDNESDAY 28**

WORD COUNT:_____   MARKETING HOURS:_____

BRAINSTORMING HOURS:_____   RESEARCH HOURS:_____

EDITING HOURS:_____   READING HOURS:_____

WEEKLY OVERVIEW

EXERCISE: Take 5-minutes to write something with the 2 words below:

Foam   Parody

Post your exercise on the 4HP Accountable Authors Group on Facebook!

What was your sprint time and top word count?

_____

List a new song you discovered this week:

_____

Favorite food or drink this week:

_____

How did you reward yourself?

_____

What project(s) did you work on?

_____

What are you reading?

_____

What went well this week?

_____

What could improve this week?

_____

_____

_____

TOTAL FOR THE WEEK

Word Count:_____   Marketing Hours:_____
Brainstorming Hours:_____   Research Hours:_____
Editing Hours:_____   Reading Hours:_____

Don't forget to color in your grid!

The Cheerleader

"Every secret of a writer's soul, every experience of his life, every quality of his mind, is written large in his works."

~ Virginia Woolf

THE ARCHITECT

Worst book to movie adaption. Eviscerate it.

THE RESEARCHER

Check your story for unnecessary characters. It seems weird, but remember, Joseph Stalin would have photos retouched to remove people who were no longer in office or died. Is there a character who doesn't support your plot or main characters? Try taking them out!

THE TASKMASTER

Don't "try" to write. Just write! It's that simple. Even if you have to put aside your current project, write a piece of flash fiction, or do another exercise--just continue to be creative.

DAILY ACCOMPLISHMENTS THURSDAY 29

WORD COUNT:_____

BRAINSTORMING HOURS:_____

EDITING HOURS:_____

MARKETING HOURS:_____

RESEARCH HOURS:_____

READING HOURS:_____

DAILY ACCOMPLISHMENTS FRIDAY 30

WORD COUNT:_____

BRAINSTORMING HOURS:_____

EDITING HOURS:_____

MARKETING HOURS:_____

RESEARCH HOURS:_____

READING HOURS:_____

THE TASKMASTER

We are nearing the end of the third quarter. Time tends to race away. It is the only commodity you can never get back. Make the most of it! As we are nearing crunch time (*aka the end of the year*), make sure you are taking time for you: a hike in the woods, a bike ride, a beer with a friend, or a bubblebath. Keeping yourself in mind will make the journey that much easier.

WEEKLY OVERVIEW

EXERCISE: Take 5-minutes to write something with the 2 words below:

Beer   Bridle

Post your exercise on the 4HP Accountable Authors Group on Facebook!

What was your sprint time and top word count?

_____

List a new song you discovered this week:

_____

Favorite food or drink this week:

_____

How did you reward yourself?

_____

What project(s) did you work on?

_____

What are you reading?

_____

What went well this week?

_____

What could improve this week?

_____

_____

_____

TOTAL FOR THE WEEK

Word Count:_____   Marketing Hours:_____
Brainstorming Hours:_____   Research Hours:_____
Editing Hours:_____   Reading Hours:_____

Don't forget to color in your grid!

SEPTEMBER

Monthly Activity Grid

SEPTEMBER

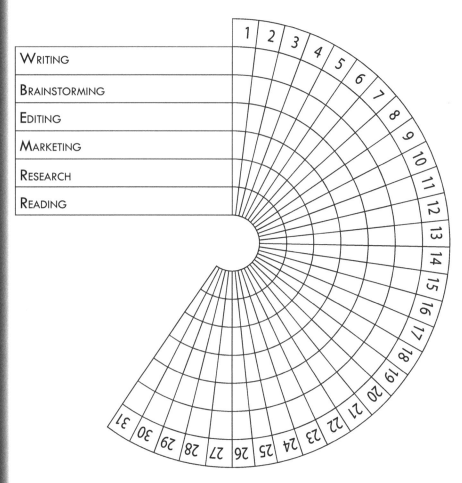

WRITING

BRAINSTORMING

EDITING

MARKETING

RESEARCH

READING

YOUR AVERAGE WORD COUNT FOR THE MONTH

Total Word Count:_____ Divided by _____ days =_____

TOTAL FOR THE YEAR SO FAR

Word Count:_____   Marketing Hours:_____
Brainstorming Hours:_____   Research Hours:_____
Editing Hours:_____   Reading Hours:_____

JOURNAL

What was your **top week**?

_____

What made your **top week** successful?

_____

What was your biggest **obstacle**?

_____

How did you **overcome** this? Or could do better next time?

_____

_____

What was your biggest **achievement**?

_____

_____

What **inspired** you most this month?

_____

Did you **discover** a new writing tip or advice this month?

_____

_____

_____

TOTAL FOR THE MONTH

Word Count:_____   Research Hours:_____
Brainstorming Hours:_____   Reading Hours:_____
Editing Hours:_____
Marketing Hours:_____

TOTAL FOR THE YEAR SO FAR

Word Count:_____   Research Hours:_____
Brainstorming Hours:_____   Reading Hours:_____
Editing Hours:_____
Marketing Hours:_____

Don't forget to color in your grid!

OCTOBER

It is the spookiest month of the year--the Muses' favorite holiday: Halloween! Besides wearing costumes and trick-or-treating, they say this is the time when the veil between worlds is the thinnest. This is the time to realize you only have three months left of 2021--and that NANO is one month away. Time to get prepared, grab a pumpkin-spiced latte and as much candy corn as you can stomach, and keep your inner demons at bay.

Oct 5 World Teachers' Day
Oct 10 Columbus Day

Oct 16 World Food Day

Oct 17 Boss's Day
Oct 31 Halloween

WHAT DOES YOUR MONTH LOOK LIKE

Holidays:_____   Weekends:_____
Weekdays:_____   Other:_____

What **project(s)** do you plan on working on?

_____

What **goal** are you aiming to achieve?

_____

What will be your biggest **obstacle** this month?

_____

How will you **overcome** this? Or adjust for this?

_____

What will be your End of the Month **reward**?

_____

GOALS FOR THIS MONTH

Word Count:_____   Marketing Hours:_____
Brainstorming Hours:_____   Research Hours:_____
Editing Hours:_____   Reading Hours:_____

OCTOBER

WEEK 1

DAILY ACCOMPLISHMENTS	**SATURDAY 1**
WORD COUNT:	MARKETING HOURS:
BRAINSTORMING HOURS:	RESEARCH HOURS:
EDITING HOURS:	READING HOURS:

DAILY ACCOMPLISHMENTS	**SUNDAY 2**
WORD COUNT:	MARKETING HOURS:
BRAINSTORMING HOURS:	RESEARCH HOURS:
EDITING HOURS:	READING HOURS:

DAILY ACCOMPLISHMENTS	**MONDAY 3**
WORD COUNT:	MARKETING HOURS:
BRAINSTORMING HOURS:	RESEARCH HOURS:
EDITING HOURS:	READING HOURS:

DAILY ACCOMPLISHMENTS	**TUESDAY 4**
WORD COUNT:	MARKETING HOURS:
BRAINSTORMING HOURS:	RESEARCH HOURS:
EDITING HOURS:	READING HOURS:

DAILY ACCOMPLISHMENTS	**WEDNESDAY 5**
WORD COUNT:	MARKETING HOURS:
BRAINSTORMING HOURS:	RESEARCH HOURS:
EDITING HOURS:	READING HOURS:

DAILY ACCOMPLISHMENTS	**THURSDAY 6**
WORD COUNT:	MARKETING HOURS:
BRAINSTORMING HOURS:	RESEARCH HOURS:
EDITING HOURS:	READING HOURS:

DAILY ACCOMPLISHMENTS	**FRIDAY 7**
WORD COUNT:	MARKETING HOURS:
BRAINSTORMING HOURS:	RESEARCH HOURS:
EDITING HOURS:	READING HOURS:

WEEKLY OVERVIEW

EXERCISE: Take 5-minutes to write something with the 2 words below:

Hallowed   Gigantic

Post your exercise on the 4HP Accountable Authors Group on Facebook!

What was your sprint time and top word count?

_____

List a new song you discovered this week:

_____

Favorite food or drink this week:

_____

How did you reward yourself?

_____

What project(s) did you work on?

_____

What are you reading?

_____

What went well this week?

_____

What could improve this week?

_____

_____

_____

TOTAL FOR THE WEEK

Word Count:_____   Marketing Hours:_____
Brainstorming Hours:_____   Research Hours:_____
Editing Hours:_____   Reading Hours:_____

Don't forget to color in your grid!

OCTOBER

The Cheerleader

Write at a different time once this week.

How did it go?

THE ARCHITECT

Search for filter words: "She saw, she heard, she noticed, etc." Then try to eliminate them as much as you can.

OCTOBER

THE RESEARCHER

Pets add agency: horses, dogs, cats, and even talking parrots. Andrew Jackson had a parrot named Polly--who cursed like a sailor to the point they removed her from his funeral! And legendary astronomer Tycho Brahe loved to get his moose drunk and let it loose!

THE TASKMASTER

If you're wondering if you're writing enough, the answer is no. Your fans want more from you. Give it to them.

OCTOBER

WEEK 2

DAILY ACCOMPLISHMENTS   SATURDAY 8

WORD COUNT:_____   MARKETING HOURS:_____
BRAINSTORMING HOURS:_____   RESEARCH HOURS:_____
EDITING HOURS:_____   READING HOURS:_____

DAILY ACCOMPLISHMENTS   SUNDAY 9

WORD COUNT:_____   MARKETING HOURS:_____
BRAINSTORMING HOURS:_____   RESEARCH HOURS:_____
EDITING HOURS:_____   READING HOURS:_____

DAILY ACCOMPLISHMENTS   MONDAY 10

WORD COUNT:_____   MARKETING HOURS:_____
BRAINSTORMING HOURS:_____   RESEARCH HOURS:_____
EDITING HOURS:_____   READING HOURS:_____

DAILY ACCOMPLISHMENTS   TUESDAY 11

WORD COUNT:_____   MARKETING HOURS:_____
BRAINSTORMING HOURS:_____   RESEARCH HOURS:_____
EDITING HOURS:_____   READING HOURS:_____

DAILY ACCOMPLISHMENTS   WEDNESDAY 12

WORD COUNT:_____   MARKETING HOURS:_____
BRAINSTORMING HOURS:_____   RESEARCH HOURS:_____
EDITING HOURS:_____   READING HOURS:_____

DAILY ACCOMPLISHMENTS   THURSDAY 13

WORD COUNT:_____   MARKETING HOURS:_____
BRAINSTORMING HOURS:_____   RESEARCH HOURS:_____
EDITING HOURS:_____   READING HOURS:_____

DAILY ACCOMPLISHMENTS   FRIDAY 14

WORD COUNT:_____   MARKETING HOURS:_____
BRAINSTORMING HOURS:_____   RESEARCH HOURS:_____
EDITING HOURS:_____   READING HOURS:_____

EXERCISE: Take 5-minutes to write something with the 2 words below:

Meaty   Afriad

Post your exercise on the 4HP Accountable Authors Group on Facebook!

What was your sprint time and top word count?

_____

List a new song you discovered this week:

_____

Favorite food or drink this week:

_____

How did you reward yourself?

_____

What project(s) did you work on?

_____

What are you reading?

_____

What went well this week?

_____

What could improve this week?

_____

_____

_____

TOTAL FOR THE WEEK

Word Count:_____   Marketing Hours:_____
Brainstorming Hours:_____   Research Hours:_____
Editing Hours:_____   Reading Hours:_____

Don't forget to color in your grid!

The Cheerleader

"Look! I have one job on this ship. It's stupid, but I'm going to do it."

~ Gwen DeMarco
(Galaxy Quest)

Nothing you write is stupid. The act of writing has meaning and value. Do your job and get those words on the page!

THE ARCHITECT

"Long patience and application saturated with your heart's blood—you will either write or you will not—and the only way to find out whether you will or not is to try."

~ Jim Tully

THE RESEARCHER

Weapons--let those guns and swords cause trouble in the plot and world. It amazes me how long a well-made blade can last. The ancient Sword of Goujian was discovered in Hubei, China after spending two millennia in a tomb. It's still razor sharp!

THE TASKMASTER

Do you believe your writing won't be appreciated by others? Well, you're wrong. If there's an audience for dinosaur romance, there are people ready to hear your story.

OCTOBER

Week 3

Daily Accomplishments — Saturday 15

Word Count:_____
Brainstorming Hours:_____
Editing Hours:_____

Marketing Hours:_____
Research Hours:_____
Reading Hours:_____

Daily Accomplishments — Sunday 16

Word Count:_____
Brainstorming Hours:_____
Editing Hours:_____

Marketing Hours:_____
Research Hours:_____
Reading Hours:_____

Daily Accomplishments — Monday 17

Word Count:_____
Brainstorming Hours:_____
Editing Hours:_____

Marketing Hours:_____
Research Hours:_____
Reading Hours:_____

Daily Accomplishments — Tuesday 18

Word Count:_____
Brainstorming Hours:_____
Editing Hours:_____

Marketing Hours:_____
Research Hours:_____
Reading Hours:_____

Daily Accomplishments — Wednesday 19

Word Count:_____
Brainstorming Hours:_____
Editing Hours:_____

Marketing Hours:_____
Research Hours:_____
Reading Hours:_____

Daily Accomplishments — Thursday 20

Word Count:_____
Brainstorming Hours:_____
Editing Hours:_____

Marketing Hours:_____
Research Hours:_____
Reading Hours:_____

Daily Accomplishments — Friday 21

Word Count:_____
Brainstorming Hours:_____
Editing Hours:_____

Marketing Hours:_____
Research Hours:_____
Reading Hours:_____

OCTOBER

Weekly Overview

EXERCISE: Take 5-minutes to write something with the 2 words below:

Silky   Unnatural

Post your exercise on the 4HP Accountable Authors Group on Facebook!

What was your sprint time and top word count?

_____

List a new song you discovered this week:

_____

Favorite food or drink this week:

_____

How did you reward yourself?

_____

What project(s) did you work on?

_____

What are you reading?

_____

What went well this week?

_____

What could improve this week?

_____

_____

_____

Total for the Week

Word Count:_____   Marketing Hours:_____
Brainstorming Hours:_____   Research Hours:_____
Editing Hours:_____   Reading Hours:_____

Don't forget to color in your grid!

The Cheerleader

Build a system! Create a money scheme, craft a calendar, draw a family tree, describe the intricacies of how a town operates, or anything else that will maintain your writing focus.

THE ARCHITECT

Interview Time: What questions would a reporter ask your hero, villain, or main character? Is it related to an even that happens in the book? Or a decision they made? Now share it!

THE RESEARCHER

"I do not over-intellectualize the production process. I try to keep it simple: Tell the damned story."

~ Tom Clancy

THE TASKMASTER

"The worst enemy to creativity is self-doubt."

~Sylvia Plath

Never doubt what you can accomplish or if it's good enough. You're doing it, and it is fantastic!

DAILY ACCOMPLISHMENTS   **SATURDAY 22**

WORD COUNT:_____ MARKETING HOURS:_____
BRAINSTORMING HOURS:_____ RESEARCH HOURS:_____
EDITING HOURS:_____ READING HOURS:_____

DAILY ACCOMPLISHMENTS   **SUNDAY 23**

WORD COUNT:_____ MARKETING HOURS:_____
BRAINSTORMING HOURS:_____ RESEARCH HOURS:_____
EDITING HOURS:_____ READING HOURS:_____

DAILY ACCOMPLISHMENTS   **MONDAY 24**

WORD COUNT:_____ MARKETING HOURS:_____
BRAINSTORMING HOURS:_____ RESEARCH HOURS:_____
EDITING HOURS:_____ READING HOURS:_____

DAILY ACCOMPLISHMENTS   **TUESDAY 25**

WORD COUNT:_____ MARKETING HOURS:_____
BRAINSTORMING HOURS:_____ RESEARCH HOURS:_____
EDITING HOURS:_____ READING HOURS:_____

DAILY ACCOMPLISHMENTS   **WEDNESDAY 26**

WORD COUNT:_____ MARKETING HOURS:_____
BRAINSTORMING HOURS:_____ RESEARCH HOURS:_____
EDITING HOURS:_____ READING HOURS:_____

DAILY ACCOMPLISHMENTS   **THURSDAY 27**

WORD COUNT:_____ MARKETING HOURS:_____
BRAINSTORMING HOURS:_____ RESEARCH HOURS:_____
EDITING HOURS:_____ READING HOURS:_____

DAILY ACCOMPLISHMENTS   **FRIDAY 28**

WORD COUNT:_____ MARKETING HOURS:_____
BRAINSTORMING HOURS:_____ RESEARCH HOURS:_____
EDITING HOURS:_____ READING HOURS:_____

OCTOBER

Weekly Overview

EXERCISE: Take 5-minutes to write something with the 2 words below:

Wanting   Collar

Post your exercise on the 4HP Accountable Authors Group on Facebook!

What was your sprint time and top word count?

_____

List a new song you discovered this week:

_____

Favorite food or drink this week:

_____

How did you reward yourself?

_____

What project(s) did you work on?

_____

What are you reading?

_____

What went well this week?

_____

What could improve this week?

_____

_____

_____

TOTAL FOR THE WEEK

Word Count:_____ Marketing Hours:_____
Brainstorming Hours:_____ Research Hours:_____
Editing Hours:_____ Reading Hours:_____

Don't forget to color in your grid!

The Cheerleader

Writing is sweat and drudgery most of the time. And you have to love it in order to endure the solitude and the discipline.

~ Peter Benchley, author of Jaws

THE ARCHITECT

Print out your work in a different font and size during revisions. The new layout will trick your brain into reading your work in a new way, making it easier to catch errors.

THE RESEARCHER

Writing on the beach or in a cabin in the woods? Pros/Cons. Are they at the most exotic beach in the world, Honopu Beach in Hawaii or the most haunted woods in the world, Aokigahara, Japan?

THE TASKMASTER

Every mistake is a learning experience. Mistakes teach us to make the same mistakes, just all new ones.

OCTOBER

DAILY ACCOMPLISHMENTS   **SATURDAY 29**

WORD COUNT:_____

BRAINSTORMING HOURS:_____

EDITING HOURS:_____

MARKETING HOURS:_____

RESEARCH HOURS:_____

READING HOURS:_____

DAILY ACCOMPLISHMENTS   **SUNDAY 30**

WORD COUNT:_____

BRAINSTORMING HOURS:_____

EDITING HOURS:_____

MARKETING HOURS:_____

RESEARCH HOURS:_____

READING HOURS:_____

DAILY ACCOMPLISHMENTS   **MONDAY 31**

WORD COUNT:_____

BRAINSTORMING HOURS:_____

EDITING HOURS:_____

MARKETING HOURS:_____

RESEARCH HOURS:_____

READING HOURS:_____

THE RESEARCHER

Your world doesn't have to make sense! Trust me, the one we live in can be unpredictable and full of strange settings. In Centraliia, Pennsylvania you can find an American ghost town. the strange part? It's had an underground fire burning for over 50 years! It started in 1962 when the town went to set fire to the local dump to "clean it up" only to set fire to the coal mine beneath the town! You can still see smoke rising through the cracks on the roads!

OCTOBER

Weekly Overview

EXERCISE: Take 5-minutes to write something with the 2 words below:

Marvelous   Cow

Post your exercise on the 4HP Accountable Authors Group on Facebook!

What was your sprint time and top word count?

_____

List a new song you discovered this week:

_____

Favorite food or drink this week:

_____

How did you reward yourself?

_____

What project(s) did you work on?

_____

What are you reading?

_____

What went well this week?

_____

What could improve this week?

_____

_____

_____

Total for the Week

Word Count:_____   Marketing Hours:_____
Brainstorming Hours:_____   Research Hours:_____
Editing Hours:_____   Reading Hours:_____

Don't forget to color in your grid!

OCTOBER

MONTHLY ACTIVITY GRID

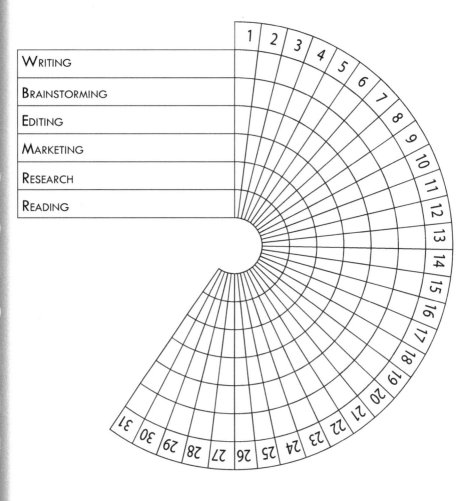

WRITING

BRAINSTORMING

EDITING

MARKETING

RESEARCH

READING

O C T O B E R

YOUR AVERAGE WORD COUNT FOR THE MONTH

Total Word Count:_____ Divided by _____ days =_____

TOTAL FOR THE YEAR SO FAR

Word Count:_____   Marketing Hours:_____
Brainstorming Hours:_____   Research Hours:_____
Editing Hours:_____   Reading Hours:_____

JOURNAL

What was your **top week**?

_____

What made your **top week** successful?

_____

What was your biggest **obstacle**?

_____

How did you **overcome** this? Or could do better next time?

_____

_____

What was your biggest **achievement**?

_____

_____

What **inspired** you most this month?

_____

Did you **discover** a new writing tip or advice this month?

_____

_____

_____

TOTAL FOR THE MONTH

Word Count:_____   Research Hours:_____
Brainstorming Hours:_____   Reading Hours:_____
Editing Hours:_____
Marketing Hours:_____

TOTAL FOR THE YEAR SO FAR

Word Count:_____   Research Hours:_____
Brainstorming Hours:_____   Reading Hours:_____
Editing Hours:_____
Marketing Hours:_____

Don't forget to color in your grid!

NOVEMBER - NANOWRIMO!

Here is where you can sign up to participate: nanowrimo.org
"EVERY STORY MATTERS." - NANOWRIMO.ORG
Let's start writing yours. Writing a novel alone can be difficult, even for seasoned writers. NaNoWriMo helps you track your progress, set milestones, connect with other writers in a vast community, and participate in events that are designed to make sure you finish your novel. Oh, and best of all, it's free!

Native American Heritage Month
Nov 1 All Saint's Day
Nov 2 All Souls' Day

Nov 8 Election Day
Nov 5 World Tsunami Awareness Day
Nov 6 Daylight Saving Time

Nov 11 Veterans Day
Nov 24 Thanksgiving
Nov 25 Black Friday

WHAT DOES YOUR MONTH LOOK LIKE

Holidays:_____   Weekends:_____

Weekdays:_____   Other:_____

What **project(s)** do you plan on working on?

_____

What **goal** are you aiming to achieve?

_____

What will be your biggest **obstacle** this month?

_____

How will you **overcome** this? Or adjust for this?

_____

What will be your End of the Month **reward**?

_____

GOALS FOR THIS MONTH

Word Count:_____   Marketing Hours:_____

Brainstorming Hours:_____   Research Hours:_____

Editing Hours:_____   Reading Hours:_____

NOVEMBER

219

Week 1

Daily Accomplishments | Tuesday 1

Word Count:_____
Brainstorming Hours:_____
Editing Hours:_____

Marketing Hours:_____
Research Hours:_____
Reading Hours:_____

Daily Accomplishments | Wednesday 2

Word Count:_____
Brainstorming Hours:_____
Editing Hours:_____

Marketing Hours:_____
Research Hours:_____
Reading Hours:_____

Daily Accomplishments | Thursday 3

Word Count:_____
Brainstorming Hours:_____
Editing Hours:_____

Marketing Hours:_____
Research Hours:_____
Reading Hours:_____

Daily Accomplishments | Friday 4

Word Count:_____
Brainstorming Hours:_____
Editing Hours:_____

Marketing Hours:_____
Research Hours:_____
Reading Hours:_____

Daily Accomplishments | Saturday 5

Word Count:_____
Brainstorming Hours:_____
Editing Hours:_____

Marketing Hours:_____
Research Hours:_____
Reading Hours:_____

Daily Accomplishments | Sunday 6

Word Count:_____
Brainstorming Hours:_____
Editing Hours:_____

Marketing Hours:_____
Research Hours:_____
Reading Hours:_____

Daily Accomplishments | Monday 7

Word Count:_____
Brainstorming Hours:_____
Editing Hours:_____

Marketing Hours:_____
Research Hours:_____
Reading Hours:_____

WEEKLY OVERVIEW

EXERCISE: Take 5-minutes to write something with the 2 words below:

Exuberant   Mom

Post your exercise on the 4HP Accountable Authors Group on Facebook!

What was your sprint time and top word count?

_____

List a new song you discovered this week:

_____

Favorite food or drink this week:

_____

How did you reward yourself?

_____

What project(s) did you work on?

_____

What are you reading?

_____

What went well this week?

_____

What could improve this week?

_____

_____

_____

TOTAL FOR THE WEEK

Word Count:_____   Marketing Hours:_____
Brainstorming Hours:_____   Research Hours:_____
Editing Hours:_____   Reading Hours:_____

Don't forget to color in your grid!

The Cheerleader

Focus on editing your work once this week. How's it coming along?

THE ARCHITECT

"Plot is people. Human emotions and desires founded on the realities of life, working at cross purposes, getting hotter and fiercer as they strike against each other until finally there's an explosion—that's Plot."

~ Leigh Brackett

THE RESEARCHER

If you want your scene to come alive for the reader, try using all of your senses: smell, sound, touch, taste, and sight. When people gather, there's always that storyteller in the group. Listen carefully how often they make sounds, or talk about the feel and smells they encountered. Even in oral format, adding senses to storytelling immerses the reader faster and hooks them to listen.

THE TASKMASTER

Believe in yourself. Decide you are a great writer--and that's exactly what you will be.

DAILY ACCOMPLISHMENTS   TUESDAY 8

WORD COUNT:_____   MARKETING HOURS:_____
BRAINSTORMING HOURS:_____   RESEARCH HOURS:_____
EDITING HOURS:_____   READING HOURS:_____

DAILY ACCOMPLISHMENTS   WEDNESDAY 9

WORD COUNT:_____   MARKETING HOURS:_____
BRAINSTORMING HOURS:_____   RESEARCH HOURS:_____
EDITING HOURS:_____   READING HOURS:_____

DAILY ACCOMPLISHMENTS   THURSDAY 10

WORD COUNT:_____   MARKETING HOURS:_____
BRAINSTORMING HOURS:_____   RESEARCH HOURS:_____
EDITING HOURS:_____   READING HOURS:_____

DAILY ACCOMPLISHMENTS   FRIDAY 11

WORD COUNT:_____   MARKETING HOURS:_____
BRAINSTORMING HOURS:_____   RESEARCH HOURS:_____
EDITING HOURS:_____   READING HOURS:_____

DAILY ACCOMPLISHMENTS   SATURDAY 12

WORD COUNT:_____   MARKETING HOURS:_____
BRAINSTORMING HOURS:_____   RESEARCH HOURS:_____
EDITING HOURS:_____   READING HOURS:_____

DAILY ACCOMPLISHMENTS   SUNDAY 13

WORD COUNT:_____   MARKETING HOURS:_____
BRAINSTORMING HOURS:_____   RESEARCH HOURS:_____
EDITING HOURS:_____   READING HOURS:_____

DAILY ACCOMPLISHMENTS   MONDAY 14

WORD COUNT:_____   MARKETING HOURS:_____
BRAINSTORMING HOURS:_____   RESEARCH HOURS:_____
EDITING HOURS:_____   READING HOURS:_____

NOVEMBER

WEEKLY OVERVIEW

EXERCISE: Take 5-minutes to write something with the 2 words below:

Throne   Maniacal

Post your exercise on the 4HP Accountable Authors Group on Facebook!

What was your sprint time and top word count?

_____

List a new song you discovered this week:

_____

Favorite food or drink this week:

_____

How did you reward yourself?

_____

What project(s) did you work on?

_____

What are you reading?

_____

What went well this week?

_____

What could improve this week?

_____

_____

_____

TOTAL FOR THE WEEK

Word Count:_____   Marketing Hours:_____
Brainstorming Hours:_____   Research Hours:_____
Editing Hours:_____   Reading Hours:_____

Don't forget to color in your grid!

The Cheerleader

"You may not always write well, but you can edit a bad page. You can't edit a blank page."
~ Jodi Picoult

THE ARCHITECT

You're in the elevator with your dream publisher. In one minute, explain why your project is freaking amazing.

THE RESEARCHER

"The greatest part of a writer's time is spent in reading, in order to write; a writer will turn over half a library to make one book."

~ Samuel Johnson

THE TASKMASTER

Stop wasting time on social media or watching Netflix. Get back to the part where you are creating worlds.

DAILY ACCOMPLISHMENTS   **TUESDAY 15**

WORD COUNT:_____   MARKETING HOURS:_____

BRAINSTORMING HOURS:_____   RESEARCH HOURS:_____

EDITING HOURS:_____   READING HOURS:_____

DAILY ACCOMPLISHMENTS   **WEDNESDAY 16**

WORD COUNT:_____   MARKETING HOURS:_____

BRAINSTORMING HOURS:_____   RESEARCH HOURS:_____

EDITING HOURS:_____   READING HOURS:_____

DAILY ACCOMPLISHMENTS   **THURSDAY 17**

WORD COUNT:_____   MARKETING HOURS:_____

BRAINSTORMING HOURS:_____   RESEARCH HOURS:_____

EDITING HOURS:_____   READING HOURS:_____

DAILY ACCOMPLISHMENTS   **FRIDAY 18**

WORD COUNT:_____   MARKETING HOURS:_____

BRAINSTORMING HOURS:_____   RESEARCH HOURS:_____

EDITING HOURS:_____   READING HOURS:_____

DAILY ACCOMPLISHMENTS   **SATURDAY 19**

WORD COUNT:_____   MARKETING HOURS:_____

BRAINSTORMING HOURS:_____   RESEARCH HOURS:_____

EDITING HOURS:_____   READING HOURS:_____

DAILY ACCOMPLISHMENTS   **SUNDAY 20**

WORD COUNT:_____   MARKETING HOURS:_____

BRAINSTORMING HOURS:_____   RESEARCH HOURS:_____

EDITING HOURS:_____   READING HOURS:_____

DAILY ACCOMPLISHMENTS   **MONDAY 21**

WORD COUNT:_____   MARKETING HOURS:_____

BRAINSTORMING HOURS:_____   RESEARCH HOURS:_____

EDITING HOURS:_____   READING HOURS:_____

NOVEMBER

WEEKLY OVERVIEW

EXERCISE: Take 5-minutes to write something with the 2 words below:

Voiceless   Tasty

Post your exercise on the 4HP Accountable Authors Group on Facebook!

What was your sprint time and top word count?

_____

List a new song you discovered this week:

_____

Favorite food or drink this week:

_____

How did you reward yourself?

_____

What project(s) did you work on?

_____

What are you reading?

_____

What went well this week?

_____

What could improve this week?

_____

_____

_____

TOTAL FOR THE WEEK

Word Count:_____   Marketing Hours:_____
Brainstorming Hours:_____   Research Hours:_____
Editing Hours:_____   Reading Hours:_____

Don't forget to color in your grid!

The Cheerleader

Post the cover of your current project on the 4HP Accountable Authors group on Facebook. Don't have one? Share one of your favorite covers and tell us why!

The Architect

Don't edit as you write. It will only slow down the drafting process. Worry about that later.

NOVEMBER

THE RESEARCHER

Take your favorite historical figures and write a Goal, Motivation, and Conflict for each of them. Do they have something in common? How does your own cast of characters compare in their own GMC charts? Bonus points if you use a historical event and evaluate all opposing sides!

THE TASKMASTER

Ctrl Find "shrug," "nod," "sigh," and any other words you use too frequently and clean that crap up!

NOVEMBER

DAILY ACCOMPLISHMENTS   TUESDAY 22

Word Count: _____   *Marketing Hours:* _____
Brainstorming Hours: _____   *Research Hours:* _____
Editing Hours: _____   *Reading Hours:* _____

DAILY ACCOMPLISHMENTS   WEDNESDAY 23

Word Count: _____   *Marketing Hours:* _____
Brainstorming Hours: _____   *Research Hours:* _____
Editing Hours: _____   *Reading Hours:* _____

DAILY ACCOMPLISHMENTS   THURSDAY 24

Word Count: _____   *Marketing Hours:* _____
Brainstorming Hours: _____   *Research Hours:* _____
Editing Hours: _____   *Reading Hours:* _____

DAILY ACCOMPLISHMENTS   FRIDAY 25

Word Count: _____   *Marketing Hours:* _____
Brainstorming Hours: _____   *Research Hours:* _____
Editing Hours: _____   *Reading Hours:* _____

DAILY ACCOMPLISHMENTS   SATURDAY 26

Word Count: _____   *Marketing Hours:* _____
Brainstorming Hours: _____   *Research Hours:* _____
Editing Hours: _____   *Reading Hours:* _____

DAILY ACCOMPLISHMENTS   SUNDAY 27

Word Count: _____   *Marketing Hours:* _____
Brainstorming Hours: _____   *Research Hours:* _____
Editing Hours: _____   *Reading Hours:* _____

DAILY ACCOMPLISHMENTS   MONDAY 28

Word Count: _____   *Marketing Hours:* _____
Brainstorming Hours: _____   *Research Hours:* _____
Editing Hours: _____   *Reading Hours:* _____

NOVEMBER

WEEKLY OVERVIEW

EXERCISE: Take 5-minutes to write something with the 2 words below:

Curve   Callous

Post your exercise on the 4HP Accountable Authors Group on Facebook!

What was your sprint time and top word count?

_____

List a new song you discovered this week:

_____

Favorite food or drink this week:

_____

How did you reward yourself?

_____

What project(s) did you work on?

_____

What are you reading?

_____

What went well this week?

_____

What could improve this week?

_____

_____

_____

TOTAL FOR THE WEEK

Word Count:_____   Marketing Hours:_____
Brainstorming Hours:_____   Research Hours:_____
Editing Hours:_____   Reading Hours:_____

Don't forget to color in your grid!

The Cheerleader

Follow two other writers on social media who are participating in Nanowrimo. If they can do it, so can you!

THE ARCHITECT

Are you telling the right character's story? Try flipping it out and write a scene from a different character's point-of-view! For example, telling a story from the POV of a shark, the diver, or even the boat can differ drastically!

NOVEMBER

THE RESEARCHER

Fun fact... Jack Kerouac never learned to drive! He relied on other means or his pal Neal Cassady to get around. Is there a character in your story who refuses or doesn't know how to do something that might force your story in a different direction? Consider adding one!

THE TASKMASTER

You are expected to fail. We will all fail many times in our lives. It's what you do with that failure that makes the difference. Learn from it.

NOVEMBER

DAILY ACCOMPLISHMENTS	TUESDAY 29
WORD COUNT:	MARKETING HOURS:
BRAINSTORMING HOURS:	RESEARCH HOURS:
EDITING HOURS:	READING HOURS:

DAILY ACCOMPLISHMENTS	WEDNESDAY 30
WORD COUNT:	MARKETING HOURS:
BRAINSTORMING HOURS:	RESEARCH HOURS:
EDITING HOURS:	READING HOURS:

The Cheerleader

"This sentence has five words. Here are five more words. Five-word sentences are fine. But several together become monotonous. Listen to what is happening. The writing is getting boring. The sound of it drones. It's like a stuck record. The ear demands some variety. Now listen. I vary the sentence length, and I create music. Music. The writing sings. It has a pleasant rhythm, a lilt, a harmony. I use short sentences. And I use sentences of medium length. And sometimes, when I am certain the reader is rested, I will engage him with a sentence of considerable length, a sentence that burns with energy and builds with all the impetus of a crescendo, the roll of the drums, the crash of the cymbals—sounds that say listen to this, it is important."

~ Gary Provost

EXERCISE: Take 5-minutes to write something with the 2 words below:

Writer   Passion

Post your exercise on the 4HP Accountable Authors Group on Facebook!

What was your sprint time and top word count?

_____

List a new song you discovered this week:

_____

Favorite food or drink this week:

_____

How did you reward yourself?

_____

What project(s) did you work on?

_____

What are you reading?

_____

What went well this week?

_____

What could improve this week?

_____

_____

_____

TOTAL FOR THE WEEK

Word Count:_____   Marketing Hours:_____
Brainstorming Hours:_____   Research Hours:_____
Editing Hours:_____   Reading Hours:_____

Don't forget to color in your grid!

NOVEMBER

Monthly Activity Grid

NOVEMBER

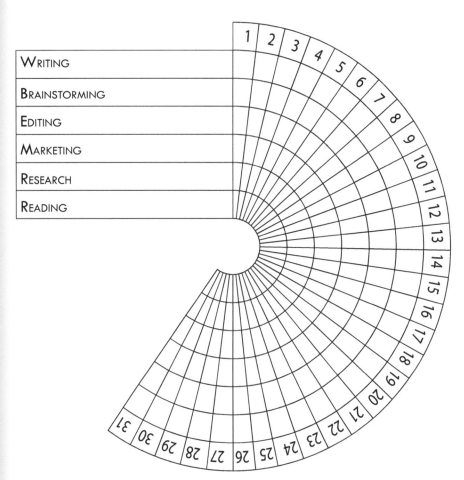

WRITING

BRAINSTORMING

EDITING

MARKETING

RESEARCH

READING

Your Average Word Count for the Month

Total Word Count:_____ Divided by _____ days =_____

Total for the Year So Far

Word Count:_____   Marketing Hours:_____
Brainstorming Hours:_____   Research Hours:_____
Editing Hours:_____   Reading Hours:_____

JOURNAL

What was your **top week**?

_____

What made your **top week** successful?

_____

What was your biggest **obstacle**?

_____

How did you **overcome** this? Or could do better next time?

_____

_____

What was your biggest **achievement**?

_____

_____

What **inspired** you most this month?

_____

Did you **discover** a new writing tip or advice this month?

_____

_____

TOTAL FOR THE MONTH

Word Count:_____   Marketing Hours:_____
Brainstorming Hours:_____   Research Hours:_____
Editing Hours:_____   Reading Hours:_____

TOTAL FOR THE YEAR SO FAR

Word Count:_____   Marketing Hours:_____
Brainstorming Hours:_____   Research Hours:_____
Editing Hours:_____   Reading Hours:_____

Don't forget to color in your grid!

DECEMBER

Okay. Breathe. You surived NANO (if you participated, and it's ok not to!). We are in the home stretch. You need to double your efforts, review your goal for the month (and year), and make sure you cross that finish line. This month is filled with distractions like food-filled holidays. Make sure you plan your productive and enjoyment time equally.

Dec 6 St. Nicholas Day
Dec 7 Pearl Harbor
Rememberance Day

Dec 15 The
Architect's Birthday
Dec 21 December Solstice
Dec 24 Christmas Eve

Dec 25 Christmas Day
Dec 31 New Year's Eve

WHAT DOES YOUR MONTH LOOK LIKE

Holidays:_____   Weekends:_____
Weekdays:_____   Other:_____

What **project(s)** do you plan on working on?

_____

What **goal** are you aiming to achieve?

_____

What will be your biggest **obstacle** this month?

_____

How will you **overcome** this? Or adjust for this?

_____

What will be your End of the Month **reward**?

_____

GOALS FOR THIS MONTH

Word Count:_____   Marketing Hours:_____
Brainstorming Hours:_____   Research Hours:_____
Editing Hours:_____   Reading Hours:_____

D E C E M B E R

WEEK 1

DAILY ACCOMPLISHMENTS	**THURSDAY 1**
WORD COUNT:	MARKETING HOURS:
BRAINSTORMING HOURS:	RESEARCH HOURS:
EDITING HOURS:	READING HOURS:

DAILY ACCOMPLISHMENTS	**FRIDAY 2**
WORD COUNT:	MARKETING HOURS:
BRAINSTORMING HOURS:	RESEARCH HOURS:
EDITING HOURS:	READING HOURS:

DAILY ACCOMPLISHMENTS	**SATURDAY 3**
WORD COUNT:	MARKETING HOURS:
BRAINSTORMING HOURS:	RESEARCH HOURS:
EDITING HOURS:	READING HOURS:

DAILY ACCOMPLISHMENTS	**SUNDAY 4**
WORD COUNT:	MARKETING HOURS:
BRAINSTORMING HOURS:	RESEARCH HOURS:
EDITING HOURS:	READING HOURS:

DAILY ACCOMPLISHMENTS	**MONDAY 5**
WORD COUNT:	MARKETING HOURS:
BRAINSTORMING HOURS:	RESEARCH HOURS:
EDITING HOURS:	READING HOURS:

DAILY ACCOMPLISHMENTS	**TUESDAY 6**
WORD COUNT:	MARKETING HOURS:
BRAINSTORMING HOURS:	RESEARCH HOURS:
EDITING HOURS:	READING HOURS:

DAILY ACCOMPLISHMENTS	**WEDNESDAY 7**
WORD COUNT:	MARKETING HOURS:
BRAINSTORMING HOURS:	RESEARCH HOURS:
EDITING HOURS:	READING HOURS:

WEEKLY OVERVIEW

EXERCISE: Take 5-minutes to write something with the 2 words below:

Ginger   Cheek

Post your exercise on the 4HP Accountable Authors Group on Facebook!

What was your sprint time and top word count?

_____

List a new song you discovered this week:

_____

Favorite food or drink this week:

_____

How did you reward yourself?

_____

What project(s) did you work on?

_____

What are you reading?

_____

What went well this week?

_____

What could improve this week?

_____

_____

_____

TOTAL FOR THE WEEK

Word Count:_____   Marketing Hours:_____
Brainstorming Hours:_____   Research Hours:_____
Editing Hours:_____   Reading Hours:_____

Don't forget to color in your grid!

The Cheerleader

"All readers come to fiction as willing accomplices to your lies. Such is the basic goodwill contract made the moment we pick up a work of fiction."

~ Steve Almond, WD

THE ARCHITECT

"One thing that helps is to give myself permission to write badly. I tell myself that I'm going to do my five or ten pages no matter what, and that I can always tear them up the following morning if I want. I'll have lost nothing—writing and tearing up five pages would leave me no further behind than if I took the day off."

~ Lawrence Block

THE RESEARCHER

My hat goes off to who kill off characters this week! I've seen this nod in several movies and books, but history shows Aeschylus died in 458 BCE when an eagle dropped a tortoise on his head, thinking his bald head was a rock! WHAT!

THE TASKMASTER

MORE WORDS!!! I'm sure if I asked, you could add a few more words on that page. I'm asking or actually, I am TELLING you. Go back in there.

DECEMBER

245

Week 2

Daily Accomplishments   **Thursday 8**

Word Count:_____   Marketing Hours:_____
Brainstorming Hours:_____ Research Hours:_____
Editing Hours:_____   Reading Hours:_____

Daily Accomplishments   **Friday 9**

Word Count:_____   Marketing Hours:_____
Brainstorming Hours:_____ Research Hours:_____
Editing Hours:_____   Reading Hours:_____

Daily Accomplishments   **Saturday 10**

Word Count:_____   Marketing Hours:_____
Brainstorming Hours:_____ Research Hours:_____
Editing Hours:_____   Reading Hours:_____

Daily Accomplishments   **Sunday 11**

Word Count:_____   Marketing Hours:_____
Brainstorming Hours:_____ Research Hours:_____
Editing Hours:_____   Reading Hours:_____

Daily Accomplishments   **Monday 12**

Word Count:_____   Marketing Hours:_____
Brainstorming Hours:_____ Research Hours:_____
Editing Hours:_____   Reading Hours:_____

Daily Accomplishments   **Tuesday 13**

Word Count:_____   Marketing Hours:_____
Brainstorming Hours:_____ Research Hours:_____
Editing Hours:_____   Reading Hours:_____

Daily Accomplishments   **Wednesday 14**

Word Count:_____   Marketing Hours:_____
Brainstorming Hours:_____ Research Hours:_____
Editing Hours:_____   Reading Hours:_____

DECEMBER

Weekly Overview

Fight   Face

Post your exercise on the 4HP Accountable Authors Group on Facebook!

What was your sprint time and top word count?

_____

List a new song you discovered this week:

_____

Favorite food or drink this week:

_____

How did you reward yourself?

_____

What project(s) did you work on?

_____

What are you reading?

_____

What went well this week?

_____

What could improve this week?

_____

_____

_____

Total for the Week

Word Count:_____   Marketing Hours:_____
Brainstorming Hours:_____   Research Hours:_____
Editing Hours:_____   Reading Hours:_____

Don't forget to color in your grid!

DECEMBER

The Cheerleader

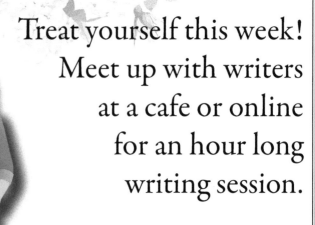

Treat yourself this week! Meet up with writers at a cafe or online for an hour long writing session.

THE ARCHITECT

Editing got you down? Try editing someone else's work or short story. This is a great way to stretch your muscles without the fog of fretting over your own prose.

DECEMBER

248

THE RESEARCHER

"Writing a book is a horrible, exhausting struggle, like a long bout of some painful illness. One would never undertake such a thing if one were not driven on by some demon whom one can neither resist nor understand."

~ George Orwell

THE TASKMASTER

Have you been practicing your book's elevator pitch? Do it some more, and polish it, even if it is not finished yet. You need to be able to say it in your sleep.

DECEMBER

DECEMBER

DAILY ACCOMPLISHMENTS — THURSDAY 15

WORD COUNT:_____
BRAINSTORMING HOURS:_____
EDITING HOURS:_____

MARKETING HOURS:_____
RESEARCH HOURS:_____
READING HOURS:_____

DAILY ACCOMPLISHMENTS — FRIDAY 16

WORD COUNT:_____
BRAINSTORMING HOURS:_____
EDITING HOURS:_____

MARKETING HOURS:_____
RESEARCH HOURS:_____
READING HOURS:_____

DAILY ACCOMPLISHMENTS — SATURDAY 17

WORD COUNT:_____
BRAINSTORMING HOURS:_____
EDITING HOURS:_____

MARKETING HOURS:_____
RESEARCH HOURS:_____
READING HOURS:_____

DAILY ACCOMPLISHMENTS — SUNDAY 18

WORD COUNT:_____
BRAINSTORMING HOURS:_____
EDITING HOURS:_____

MARKETING HOURS:_____
RESEARCH HOURS:_____
READING HOURS:_____

DAILY ACCOMPLISHMENTS — MONDAY 19

WORD COUNT:_____
BRAINSTORMING HOURS:_____
EDITING HOURS:_____

MARKETING HOURS:_____
RESEARCH HOURS:_____
READING HOURS:_____

DAILY ACCOMPLISHMENTS — TUESDAY 20

WORD COUNT:_____
BRAINSTORMING HOURS:_____
EDITING HOURS:_____

MARKETING HOURS:_____
RESEARCH HOURS:_____
READING HOURS:_____

DAILY ACCOMPLISHMENTS — WEDNESDAY 21

WORD COUNT:_____
BRAINSTORMING HOURS:_____
EDITING HOURS:_____

MARKETING HOURS:_____
RESEARCH HOURS:_____
READING HOURS:_____

Weekly Overview

EXERCISE: Take 5-minutes to write something with the 2 words below:

Birthmark   Victory

Post your exercise on the 4HP Accountable Authors Group on Facebook!

What was your sprint time and top word count?

_____

List a new song you discovered this week:

_____

Favorite food or drink this week:

_____

How did you reward yourself?

_____

What project(s) did you work on?

_____

What are you reading?

_____

What went well this week?

_____

What could improve this week?

_____

_____

_____

Total for the Week

Word Count:_____   Marketing Hours:_____
Brainstorming Hours:_____   Research Hours:_____
Editing Hours:_____   Reading Hours:_____

Don't forget to color in your grid!

The Cheerleader

The Doctor Is In: What struggles are your characters facing right now? Work through the issues here.

THE ARCHITECT

"Write. Rewrite. When not writing or rewriting, read. I know of no shortcuts."

~ Larry L. King

DECEMBER

THE RESEARCHER

Have you identified your character's neighbors? Didn't think about it? Here's a fun fact... Harriet Beecher Stowe, author of Uncle Tom's Cabin, lived next door to Mark Twain! WHAT! Sometimes help is just one knock away. Time to go borrow some sugar!

THE TASKMASTER

Editors are your friends. They are not your nice friends. They can be downright mean sometimes. They are simply making your work better. Remember that.

DECEMBER

253

DAILY ACCOMPLISHMENTS **THURSDAY 22**

WORD COUNT: _____ *MARKETING HOURS:* _____
BRAINSTORMING HOURS: _____ *RESEARCH HOURS:* _____
EDITING HOURS: _____ *READING HOURS:* _____

DAILY ACCOMPLISHMENTS **FRIDAY 23**

WORD COUNT: _____ *MARKETING HOURS:* _____
BRAINSTORMING HOURS: _____ *RESEARCH HOURS:* _____
EDITING HOURS: _____ *READING HOURS:* _____

DAILY ACCOMPLISHMENTS **SATURDAY 24**

WORD COUNT: _____ *MARKETING HOURS:* _____
BRAINSTORMING HOURS: _____ *RESEARCH HOURS:* _____
EDITING HOURS: _____ *READING HOURS:* _____

DAILY ACCOMPLISHMENTS **SUNDAY 25**

WORD COUNT: _____ *MARKETING HOURS:* _____
BRAINSTORMING HOURS: _____ *RESEARCH HOURS:* _____
EDITING HOURS: _____ *READING HOURS:* _____

DAILY ACCOMPLISHMENTS **MONDAY 26**

WORD COUNT: _____ *MARKETING HOURS:* _____
BRAINSTORMING HOURS: _____ *RESEARCH HOURS:* _____
EDITING HOURS: _____ *READING HOURS:* _____

DAILY ACCOMPLISHMENTS **TUESDAY 27**

WORD COUNT: _____ *MARKETING HOURS:* _____
BRAINSTORMING HOURS: _____ *RESEARCH HOURS:* _____
EDITING HOURS: _____ *READING HOURS:* _____

DAILY ACCOMPLISHMENTS **WEDNESDAY 28**

WORD COUNT: _____ *MARKETING HOURS:* _____
BRAINSTORMING HOURS: _____ *RESEARCH HOURS:* _____
EDITING HOURS: _____ *READING HOURS:* _____

DECEMBER

Weekly Overview

EXERCISE: Take 5-minutes to write something with the 2 words below:

Disposition   Unexpected

Post your exercise on the 4HP Accountable Authors Group on Facebook!

What was your sprint time and top word count?

_____

List a new song you discovered this week:

_____

Favorite food or drink this week:

_____

How did you reward yourself?

_____

What project(s) did you work on?

_____

What are you reading?

_____

What went well this week?

_____

What could improve this week?

_____

_____

_____

Total for the Week

Word Count:_____   Marketing Hours:_____
Brainstorming Hours:_____   Research Hours:_____
Editing Hours:_____   Reading Hours:_____

Don't forget to color in your grid!

The Cheerleader

""To gain your own voice, you have to forget about having it heard."
~ Allen Ginsberg, WD

"

THE ARCHITECT

Swap a chapter or short story with a critique partner and edit. What do you like about their style? Where can they improve? How is your writing different?

THE RESEARCHER

"Who wants to become a writer? And why? Because it's the answer to everything. ... It's the streaming reason for living. To note, to pin down, to build up, to create, to be astonished at nothing, to cherish the oddities, to let nothing go down the drain, to make something, to make a great flower out of life, even if it's a cactus."

~ Enid Bagnold

THE TASKMASTER

Hero to Zero. Start each day with a goal. When you achieve it, celebrate for a moment, then start again.

DECEMBER

257

DAILY ACCOMPLISHMENTS	**THURSDAY 29**
WORD COUNT:	*MARKETING HOURS:*
BRAINSTORMING HOURS:	*RESEARCH HOURS:*
EDITING HOURS:	*READING HOURS:*

DAILY ACCOMPLISHMENTS	**FRIDAY 30**
WORD COUNT:	*MARKETING HOURS:*
BRAINSTORMING HOURS:	*RESEARCH HOURS:*
EDITING HOURS:	*READING HOURS:*

DAILY ACCOMPLISHMENTS	**SATURDAY 31**
WORD COUNT:	*MARKETING HOURS:*
BRAINSTORMING HOURS:	*RESEARCH HOURS:*
EDITING HOURS:	*READING HOURS:*

THE ARCHITECT
How would you describe your writing style?
Pantser, Plotter, or Plantser?

I hope you consider yourself a badass! I know I do. YOU DID IT! You made it to the end of this book. Now grab next year's version and start again.

DECEMBER

WEEKLY OVERVIEW

EXERCISE: Take 5-minutes to write something with the 2 words below:

Wine   Goal

Post your exercise on the 4HP Accountable Authors Group on Facebook!

What was your sprint time and top word count?

_____

List a new song you discovered this week:

_____

Favorite food or drink this week:

_____

How did you reward yourself?

_____

What project(s) did you work on?

_____

What are you reading?

_____

What went well this week?

_____

What could improve this week?

_____

_____

_____

TOTAL FOR THE WEEK

Word Count:_____   Marketing Hours:_____
Brainstorming Hours:_____   Research Hours:_____
Editing Hours:_____   Reading Hours:_____

Don't forget to color in your grid!

MONTHLY ACTIVITY GRID

DECEMBER

WRITING OR WORD COUNT

BRAINSTORMING

EDITING

MARKETING OR SOCIAL MEDIA

RESEARCH

READING

OTHER:

1 2 3 4 5 6 7 8 9 10 11 12 13 14 15 16 17 18 19 20 21 22 23 24 25 26 27 28 29 30 31

YOUR AVERAGE WORD COUNT FOR THE MONTH

Total Word Count:_____ Divided by _____ days =_____

TOTAL FOR THE YEAR

Word Count:_____   Marketing Hours:_____
Brainstorming Hours:_____   Research Hours:_____
Editing Hours:_____   Reading Hours:_____

JOURNAL

What was your **top week**?

_____

What made your **top week** successful?

_____

What was your biggest **obstacle**?

_____

How did you **overcome** this? Or could do better next time?

_____

_____

What was your biggest **achievement**?

_____

_____

What **inspired** you most this month?

_____

Did you **discover** a new writing tip or advice this month?

_____

_____

D E C E M B E R

TOTAL FOR THE MONTH

Word Count:_____   Marketing Hours:_____
Brainstorming Hours:_____   Research Hours:_____
Editing Hours:_____   Reading Hours:_____

TOTAL FOR THE YEAR SO FAR

Word Count:_____   Marketing Hours:_____
Brainstorming Hours:_____   Research Hours:_____
Editing Hours:_____   Reading Hours:_____

Don't forget to color in your grid!

The year is
Officially OVER!

Great job
staying accountable!

Time for your
Yearly Review!

YEARLY GRID BY ACTIVITY

N ow, let's see what your activity looks like! This grid is designed to reveal what activities you do most in regards to the month or season even. You may be surprised that you do more writing at the start or end of the year. Take a moment and really pay attention to what you did, when you did it, and how you can best set your goals for the next year!

☐	WRITING
☐	BRAINSTORMING
☐	EDITING
☐	MARKETING
☐	RESEARCH
☐	READING
☐	OTHER:
☐	OTHER:
☐	OTHER:

YOUR AVERAGE WORD COUNT FOR THE YEAR

Total Word Count:_____ Divided by 365 =_____

What area did you spend the most time on?

_____

_____

What area should you work on n?

_____

_____

	J	F	M	A	M	J	J	A	S	O	N	D
1												
2												
3												
4												
5												
6												
7												
8												
9												
10												
11												
12												
13												
14												
15												
16												
17												
18												
19												
20												
21												
22												
23												
24												
25												
26												
27												
28												
29		■										
30		■										
31		■		■		■			■		■	

YEARLY GRID BY PROJECT

Let's take a look at your projects. If you were wondering why we were asking about this, we want to not only wanted to hold you accountable, but reveal some insight on how long it takes to complete them and how much of your year was spent on each one. Self-evaluation is important for prepping your goals for the year to come and also reveals about how much you really can do in the time you have. You might surprise yourself with the end result here!

☐	_____
☐	_____
☐	_____
☐	_____
☐	_____
☐	_____
☐	_____
☐	_____
☐	_____
☐	_____

What project did you spend the most time on?

_____

_____

Was this a bigger project or more difficult to complete?

_____

_____

	J	F	M	A	M	J	J	A	S	O	N	D
1												
2												
3												
4												
5												
6												
7												
8												
9												
10												
11												
12												
13												
14												
15												
16												
17												
18												
19												
20												
21												
22												
23												
24												
25												
26												
27												
28												
29		■										
30		■										
31		■		■		■			■		■	

THE YEAR IN REVIEW

THE RECKONING

How did you do? Did you do better or worse than expected?

_____

What prize or punishment did you award yourself?

_____

CAPTURE THE NOW

How do you feel right now?

_____

What are you wearing right now, Jake from State Farm? Where are you? Record this moment for Future You to enjoy.

_____

REFLECTION TIME

What habits or practices worked for you this year? Why do you think those worked for you?

_____

What obstacles did you struggle to overcome? How can you address those in the future?

_____

What lessons did you learn this year?

_____

FINAL THOUGHTS

Advice for your Former Self: What would you say now to Old You?

_____

Advice for your Future Self: What would you say to Future You?

_____

TOP TEN

> *"And remember, this is for posterity, so...be honest."*
> *--Count Rugen (The Princess Bride)*

1. Best song:_____

2. Best TV show:_____

3. Best movie:_____

4. Best book:_____

5. Best writing moment:_____

6. Best dialogue line:_____

7. Best tips/advice:_____

8. Best life moment:_____

9. Best writing spot:_____

10. Best drink/food:_____

So I Failed...Now What?

Y ou keep writing, that's what you do. Get back on the path and keep going. But it's probably a good time to reevaluate your goals. What is a more reasonable goal for you? Think about the reasons that caused you to fail this time. What can you do differently next time? What are some unanticipated issues you ran into this time? Why didn't you think they would be obstacles? What can you do to prevent more obstacles from knocking you off the writing path?

So I'm finished...Now What?

Y ay!!! Cheer one more time for the level of amazingness that is you! Enjoy that sweet reward. You earned this. Relish the moment. Remember this feeling. (Maybe even write down how you feel right now, so you can remind Future You of what is possible.) Now, set the bar a little higher and push yourself to grow or attempt to hit the same goals twice in a row!

Keep that magic going. Keep doing what worked for you this time, and use it to write the next project. Create new rewards and punishments. Plan a new project. Get lost in another world that demands to be poured onto the page. Take note of what worked and what didn't. Like, literally write it down. Use those notes as a record of your writing journey. People change, and so does writing. Allow yourself to see the path you've been on (while looking forward to what comes next).

NEXT YEAR PREP

What projects do you want to complete next year?

_____

_____

_____

_____

_____

Make your Reading List for next year.

_____

_____

_____

_____

_____

Stay accountable

and grab the next edition!